MARIA CALLAS

HALL OF FAME

MARIA CALLAS

HALL OF FAME

Giandonato Crico

GREMESE

"Hall of Fame" series
*Monographs on the performing
arts for school and university*

PHOTOGRAPHY CREDITS

Publifoto (p.6), *Dufoto Archives* (pp. 2, 8 right, 10 below right, 34, 37, 40, 41, 42, 43, 49, 51 above right, 54 above left, 59, 60, 61, 65, 70, 76, 78 right), *Mondadori Centre of Documentation* (pp. 8 above left, 79), *Gli Olmi Archives* (pp. 8 centre and below left, 10 above left, 45,) Association *"Maria Callas"* (cover, pp. 11, 12, 14, 16, 18 left [photo Locchi], 20, 22, 24 [Reale Photographic Giacomelli], 26, 46, 54 below right, 55, 57, 62, 68), *Farabolafoto* (p.13). The photos on cover and pages 18 (right), 22, 25 (right), 26, 29, 32, 34, 38, 39, 44, 45, 52, 54, 72 and 74 are by E. Piccagliani, La Scala Theater.

As far as possible the Publisher has tried to find the name of the photographers whose photographs are published in this volume, in order to attribute them correctly. However, this research has not always been successful and therefore the Publisher apologizes for any possible errors opr omissions. In the event of reprinting the Publisher declares himself ready to meake any necessary correction and to recognize any rights, according to article 70, from law number 633, 1941.

Translation:
Charles Nopar, with the collaboration of Sandra Tokunaga

Cover:
Maria Callas, *Traviata*, La Scala Theater, 1955

Cover design:
graphic office "apostoli & maggi" – Rome

Phototypeset:
Graphic Art 6 s.r.l. – Rome

Printed and bound:
C.S.R. – Rome

© 2000 – E. GREMESE EDITORE s.r.l. – Rome

*All rights reserved. No part of this book may be reproduced,
recorded or transmitted in any way or by any means
without the prior consent of the Publisher.*

ISBN 88-7301-394-5

INDEX

INTRODUCTION 7
THE BEGINNINGS 9
THE BIRTH OF A LEGEND 17
CALLAS-VISCONTI 27
THE WORLD AND ROME 37
THE NEW LIFE 47
BEFORE SILENCE 55
THE RETURN 67
THE TIME OF MEMORY 73

The Recordings 77

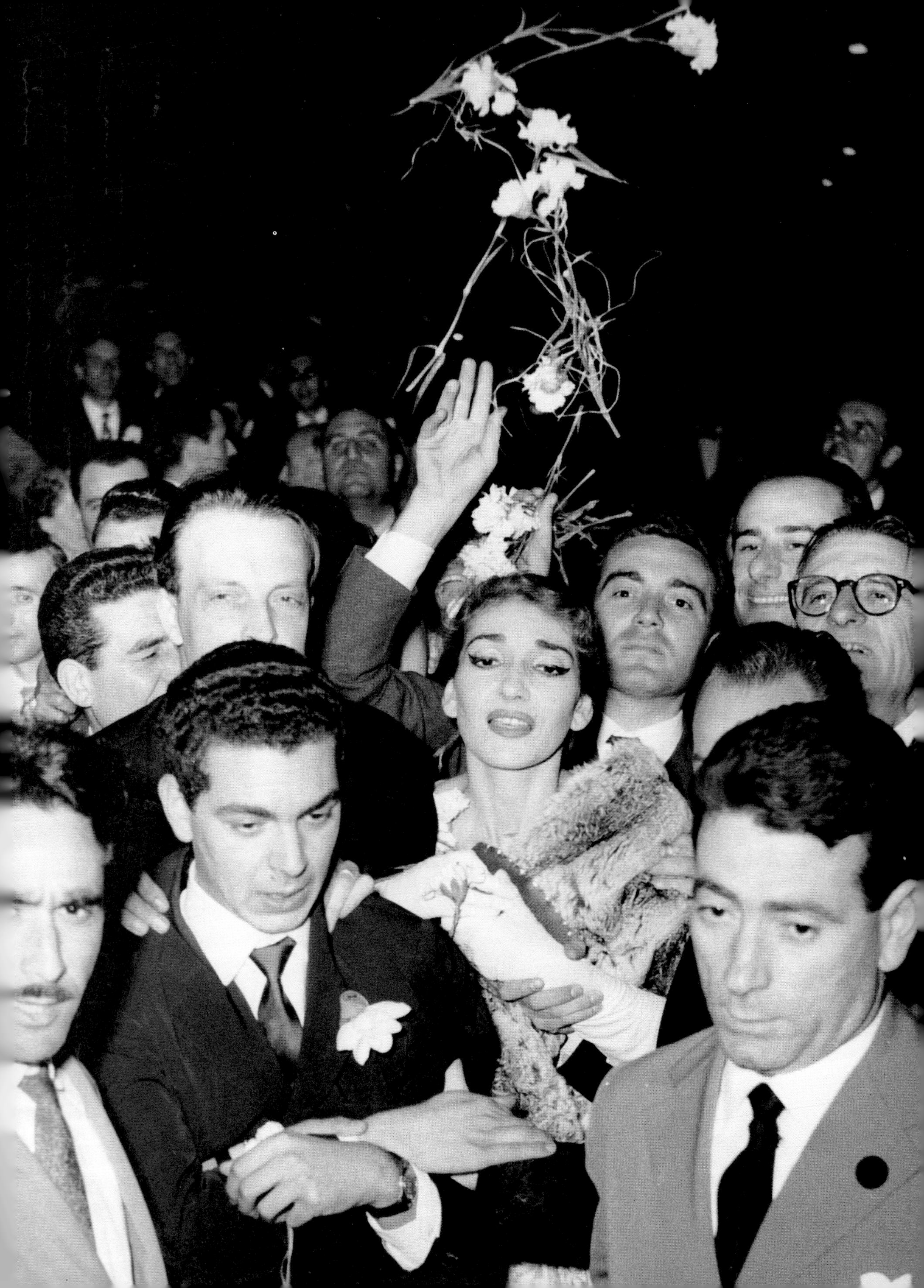

INTRODUCTION

Few women in the course of the twentieth century have aroused so much interest and excitement as Maria Callas. An indestructible myth for millions of opera goers throughout the world, a cult figure who sometimes became an object of idolatry worthy of a rock star for generations of enthusiasts, her face, her voice and her legend are one of the cultural icons of our times. More than twenty years after her death, her name is still alive all over the world, known even to those who perhaps have no very precise idea of who Maria Callas really was and perhaps have never heard a recording of her singing.

Callas, in short, like Garbo: the sheer magic of a name to which one might confidently apply the famous definition Jean Cocteau gave to Marlene Dietrich's: "A name that begins like a caress and finishes with a whip lash".

But who truly was Maria Callas? A Greek child born in New York, an adolescent with complexes, humiliated by the excessive beauty of a sister, a young fat and shapeless singer with the gift of an equally abnormal and peerless voice.

And then, almost overnight, without any transition, a diva of international prestige, the muse of the greatest intellects of her time, an angular and elegant woman launched into the international jet set, a magazine idol because of her loves, friendships, scandals and demonic rages.

"Divina" as they shout in the theaters when she sings and always a diva in her slightest actions. One of those voice-women who seem to burst into flame by spontaneous combustion each time they appear before the footlights, inflaming the audience and consuming themselves more and more each time until dying from it. Just as in other circles did Judy Garland or Edith Piaf.

On these blazing fires, on this devouring capacity for exaltation, is the Callas legend based, for those who know it. For the others it is worthwhile learning her story.

The childhood, adolescence and early youth of Cecilia Sofia Anna Maria Kalogeropoulos, not yet known as Maria Callas.

THE BEGINNINGS

New York, December 1923. In a hospital room, a Greek immigrant, Evangelia Dimitriadis, married to the pharmacist Georges Kalogeropoulos, refuses three days running to see the little girl who has just been born to her. Perhaps that pregnancy had been undesired, perhaps having another girl was a disappointment to her, or perhaps the death of little Vassili, carried off by typhoid fever was too recent to allow for consolation.

However that may be, the little girl (actually a tall and robust baby) Cecilia Sofia Anna Maria (later Mary Ann and once back in Athens, Marianna) was immediately treated to a form of rejection that was to condition her character and behavior all the years of her life. Her family had arrived in New York only a few months earlier, abandoning a comfortable economic situation, a patriarchal kind of family full of music lovers and musicians, but also the horror of the child who had died at only one year of age, the memory of which in the place where it had all happened, risked becoming a kind of obsession.

But New York is no easy city and in those years it was harder still. The style in which the Kalogeropoulos couple had been used to living was forced to become rather more modest and this did not please Evangelia one little bit. Especially because there was the first born girl in the house, she too with her name Americanized into Jackie, who was elegant and a beauty with a strong gift for music. Thus Jackie had to have her piano lessons and, pretty as she was, they had to be able to buy her clothes worthy of her.

Maria definitely took a back seat in all of this. Not that she was ugly, but she was by no means a Jackie. She was tall and dark with heavier features (like her mother's), very myopic, a greedy eater and full of complexes with a certain tendency to putting on too much weight. She also liked music, enjoying rather too much, though, listening to the radio and singing everything she heard from opera to musicals to popular songs, much to Evangelia's exasperation. And by dint of hearing her daughter sing Carmen and Philine, Aida and "La Paloma" she was turned into the typical "American mommy".

So Maria was forced into having lessons,

I owe much to Bizet. It was his Carmen *that first fascinated me, perhaps determined my life. I went, I recall, from one room of the house to another repeating the provocative habanera.*

My sister was a beautiful girl, but I was really fat and full of pimples. I was always old beyond my years — and not very happy. I had no young friends, but I had this sister who was so beautiful that I was undoubtedly the ugly duckling.

New York – Athens and back with uncertainties about the future.

even if economical ones, entering radio contests, and doing her stuff at the many Greek community celebrations on Long Island. Until one day Evangelia, fed up with New York, with her husband, with having to live a life she considers inadequate, decides to take the girls home to Greece so "the family could get to know them". No sooner said than done: they cross the ocean, reach Greece, are reinserted into the bosom of the family and have no intention of ever going back. It is 1937 and Maria is 14. The whole family holds a meeting and decides that Maria must study singing. So she gains admittance to the conservatory despite being under age, studies with Maria Trivella and immediately class concerts begin. She also sings Santuzza in *Cavalleria Rusticana* and, however amateurish the whole thing may be, gets to do the role at only sixteen.

The years in Greece are the object of some controversy in the life of Maria Callas. Was she really feeling as miserable as her biographers like to insist? Indeed many, beginning with she herself, say yes. Fat, ugly (with a nose that in adolescence had grown "important" to say the least), neglected by her family, frustrated by comparisons with a Jackie always prettier, elegant and making all the right moves, including a prestigious engagement… Maybe, but photos often show us a smiling girl clearly at ease among her friends. Still a little heavy in the hips and legs, it is true, but certainly not obese; moon-faced on occasion if you like, but interesting looking. Her myopia is strong, but her eyes are lovely, large and mature.

Then too, she undoubtedly has a voice and it too is mature and unusually big. A large voice all still to be put right, raw and unruly, but impressive in size. Maria gives it all her attention. Study totally absorbs her and gives her the balance and confidence that she may not find at home. She has met Elvira de Hidalgo, a singer still young-looking at forty-seven, but no longer active although with an electrifying career behind her: Paris, Vienna, La Scala, New York, all of Europe and Chicago. Twenty years spent at the top in light soprano and coloratura roles. De Hidalgo, friendly and lively, having gone over to teaching, hears Maria and takes her on as a student.

She became Maria's second mother, her friend, her rigorous and impassioned teacher. Is Maria's voice impressive and raw? Then she would take up the task of making it fluid and faster. To do this she has a stroke of genius: train that voice which weighs tons as

With her colleagues on the set of Fidelio.

THE BEGINNINGS

> *My vocal timbre was dark, blackish (when I think about it, a greasy oil comes to mind) and complicated by limits in the top register.*

a coloratura soprano: scales, trills, arpeggios, staccati and ornaments of every kind so that it will acquire speed and precision, become clean and light.

With de Hildago's teaching, Maria finds what she needs: concentration, study, goals to be achieved, obstacles to be overcome. She is stubborn and studious to a fault, terribly devoted to that woman who gives her voice wings. (And she will remain devoted to her until the end, going back to study with her when it seems she no longer has her voice, when her career appears to be over for good, at the end of the sixties. De Hildago outlived her by three years.)

Above all else, Maria sings – in a student environment and elsewhere. She sings until the very threshold of the war and she continues trying to sing despite the hostilities, for the Italians, the Germans, probably without thinking much about who is in her audience as long as she can be on the stage. And no matter how few the opportunities, she sings everything: concerts at the conservatory, a little Puccini (*Suor Angelica* and, at nineteen, *Tosca*), a bit of operetta, sacred music (even Pergolesi's *Stabat Mater*), German opera (*Tiefland*) and Greek, whatever is possible in a country at war, defeated and occupied. In August 1944 she triumphs in *Fidelio*, performed at the amphitheater of Herod Atticus before Nazi troops. By now she is in a position where jealousy and revenge are easily aroused.

She is only just twenty-one and is given privileges that older, more expert singers deem excessive. She is accused of collaboration, unpleasant rumors make the rounds, some colleagues treat her with hostility. For the rest, if during her formative

Elvira de Hildago, Callas' beloved teacher of the Athens years.

years and later during the war she sang whatever she came across, when the war ended, she wondered whether the Athens Opera was really the theater she wanted to stay at. Better to try America since father was still there.

> *I like working, it is always lovely to work, it is what truly entertains me.*

Her first steps in Italy singing the most challenging roles. Here she plays the blonde Isolde.

A rotten choice. It would have been better to go straight to Italy as de Hidalgo had insisted. But instead, she gets a ship that is hardly more than a cattle carrier, a never-ending crossing and finally: New York. The bell rings for the start of the fight. New York wins round one. On the plus side is the reunion with a gentle and affectionate father – but otherwise…? No one is the least interested in her successes in Greece and there are no opportunities for work. A failed audition to sing *Madam Butterfly* at the Met (if one must try, why not aim for the top at once?); a misfired encounter with a new singing teacher who mainly works to increase the size of her voice; an unlucky lead to Chicago for a post-war season that does not come off and so wastes her time and efforts to learn *Turandot*; and frustrating contacts with the inevitably squalid underbrush of the music world.

Amidst so much desolation, one ray of sunshine (and Maria has gained a lot of weight, too much weight, in moving from one disappointment to the next): the young bass Nicola Rossi Lemeni, who was also involved in the failed Chicago adventure, gives her name to Giovanni Zenatello. This once famous tenor, now artistic director of the Arena of Verona, has come to New York looking for a Gioconda for the coming summer season. He has already engaged Rossi Lemeni and agrees to give an audition to the soprano whom Lemeni has recommended. Maria's singing convinces him, even makes him enthusiastic: he will give her a debutante's cachet, will not pay her trip, but guarantees her an audience of 20,000 spectators an evening for five performances.

Furthermore, her conductor will be the great Serafin, who will also be in charge of *Faust* with another very young debutante: Renata Tebaldi – recommended by no one less than Arturo Toscanini. Maria, who has not sung in public since September 1945, does not think twice. She will find the money for the trip and signs. Another ship more like a cattle carrier and another endless ocean voyage. Then, from Naples, the exhausting change to a train in hot and battered Italy.

And finally, Verona, beautiful and gentle, civilized and restful. The Piazza Bra, the restaurants on the Liston: a different air to breathe, a different style of life. Then the encounters with famous colleagues, the rehearsals. Serafin from the class of 1878, with his white mane and international experience and incontestable prestige. An orchestra conductor who has conducted everyone, but really every one of the world's great singers and, in particular, Rosa Ponselle whom Maria as a child had loved so much.

Now it is her turn, her chance. The *Gioconda* at the Arena is usually taken to be the turning point in Maria's career, but it is not as if everything had settled into place in that

> *She was a born heroine.*
> *Neither beautiful nor ugly.*
> *She was what she was, that's all,*
> *outside the categories. Her mouth*
> *was enormous, her nose bent down,*
> *but those immense, incredible eyes*
> *in which one lost oneself.*
> GIULIETTA SIMIONATO

summer of '47 with the waving of a magic wand. Maria sang her five performances with passion, certainly, but with success…? All in all, yes, but not as if they had left indelible traces. At least not yet. In any case, no one made her any offers.

No contracts, no leads. Maria might as well have gone back to the States if it had not been… if it had not been for another hoary head who shows up at the restaurants on the Liston – Giovanni Battista Meneghini, a friendly likable man in his fifties in the construction materials industry who takes a shine to her. So much of a shine, that he not only invites her on a lovely trip to Venice, but in those few days, can no longer tear himself from her side, proposes marriage and also offers to take charge of her career. Maria accepts. Gentleness, devotion, protection, economic security are all values to which she cannot be indifferent and the *commendatore* offers them all with simplicity. Furthermore, his intentions are sincere, there can be no doubts about that.

Little by little, Maria's career makes headway. It is true that she has to wait four months before stepping onto another stage, but on December 30 in Venice she sings her first Isolde at the Wagnerian opening of La Fenice, and in the following year she has only June for relaxing. During the other months she makes the rounds of Venice, Udine, Trieste, Genoa, Rome, Verona once more, Turin, Rovigo and Florence… about thirty performances, not more, but at regular intervals with many *Turandots* and then *Aida*, *La Forza del destino*, and her first *Norma*.

These are months in which Maria is finding herself, accepting possibly whatever is offered – and these are often contracts signed as they come without any real planning. But Maria is singing, earning money, and acquiring the esteem of Serafin who, after the first Venice *Tristan*, wants her for the Genoa production as well, and then in *Aida* and *Norma*. He is the guiding figure of her first Italian years.

Up until 1952 he conducts her performances of *Die Walküre*, *Puritani*, *Parsifal*, *Traviata*, *Trovatore* and *Armida*. He will also be by her side in almost all her recordings up until 1960 and Maria will forever show him unwavering esteem and deference, affection, and the greatest gratitude. The same gratitude that she feels for Meneghini – known familiarly as Titta or, Veronese style, Tita – and which little by little turns into love.

One of the first and florid editions of La Traviata.

They marry in Verona in 1949. For ten years they are inseparable. She, utterly concentrated on her career, and he, mostly involved in managing the financial end of it. A curious couple with their 26-year age difference, the difference in character and propensities, and yet incontestably a solid relationship according to the testimony of their friends, colleagues and acquaintances. Meanwhile, during those first years, Maria makes a name for herself in Italy and South America. Between 1949 and 1952 she sings every season in Buenos Aires, Mexico City, São Paolo and Rio de Janeiro – warm-hearted cities with torrid opera fans where her evenings turn at times into vocal athletic events looking to unleash the wildest applause and deafening ovations.

Those South American nights are ones which sometimes push her beyond the brink, when she indulges herself in real vocal follies. (On a bet one evening she closes the second act ensemble of *Aida* with a high E that, like a lightening flash, breaks through the *fortissimo* sound barrier of the other soloists, chorus and orchestra). But these are also evenings where she unveils apparently unlimited vocal resources of a kind to arouse the spite of colleagues both male and female. To those evenings, possibly a little too colorful, we owe the dissension to tenors out-sung and invidious basses. The war of the encores also turns her relationship rigid with such a colleague as Renata Tebaldi, up until then friendly and full of reciprocal admiration.

The fact is that Maria is possessed by the need to excel, the desire for vindication, the awareness of being artistically exceptional even if not yet entirely disciplined. This leads her to attitudes that can appear – and perhaps really are – egotistical, if not downright disdainful, to the detriment of diplomacy and her relationship with the public. In Italy, however, Maria makes at least two important conquests: Venice, which offers her the first big chances, and Florence where she sings *Norma* and *Traviata* for the first time and

Still over weight, Maria Callas has learned to put the emphasis on her eyes.

The Beginnings

> *I have no recollection of serene performances. Each time I had to win over the public note by note.*

where she soon presents her legendary interpretations of *Armida* and *Medea*.

There is also Rome which, following her *Turandot* at Caracalla in 1948, offers her five roles in the three following years. Then there are other theaters, all of them important (minor towns saw little of her: Udine, Rovigo, Brescia, Pisa, Reggio Calabria, Cagliari, Bergamo and Ravenna between 1948 and 1954). In short, if she had ever been part of the Italian ranks, her rise was very fast.

The theaters understood at once – with the help of Serafin's unimpeachable seal of approval – that this strange voice could be made to sing practically anything. But her impact on the public and the critics was not always a happy one. Maria's voice was impressive, to be sure (and always was from when she first began to study); but it was so far outside the norms as to irritate not a few people, especially in a country where "a beautiful voice" was considered foremost.

The reviewers, in fact, are not unanimous and certain critics go at her quite relentlessly. This was because she still had not truly found herself, and though she sang everything from Rossini to Wagner, from Bellini to *Tosca*, she persevered in her studying, trying to put right that which by nature was not perfectly balanced. She was also going through a difficult physical phase: having put on a lot of weight she looked bloated; she had skin and circulation problems; she was neglecting herself, dressing badly, with her make-up looking even worse. Her abominable little hats gave her the air of an elderly housewife if not just downright horrible. Her enemies derided her for this too and she suffered from it.

Her adolescent complexes of being outshone by her sister Jackie's blonde radiance, if ever they had disappeared, now returned. The insecurity caused by her ever worsening myopia also reappeared (for which her heavy, thick glasses served as a screen). Once again she sought vindication in work: she studied, nurtured her awareness of being unique, called on the teachings of de Hildago, vocalized, practiced, tried again by herself or with her coach, at all hours, even when others had not yet arrived or had already left.

She got herself an impregnable reputation as a true professional, winning the esteem of the whole troupe, the respect of the chorus. She showed that she could sing the most varied parts in diverse tessituras. She *must* do more and better than the others. And fortunately, she began finding people everywhere who seemed to have eyes only for her, who considered her unique and were determined to say so.

Kundry, one of the Wagnerian roles of her early career.

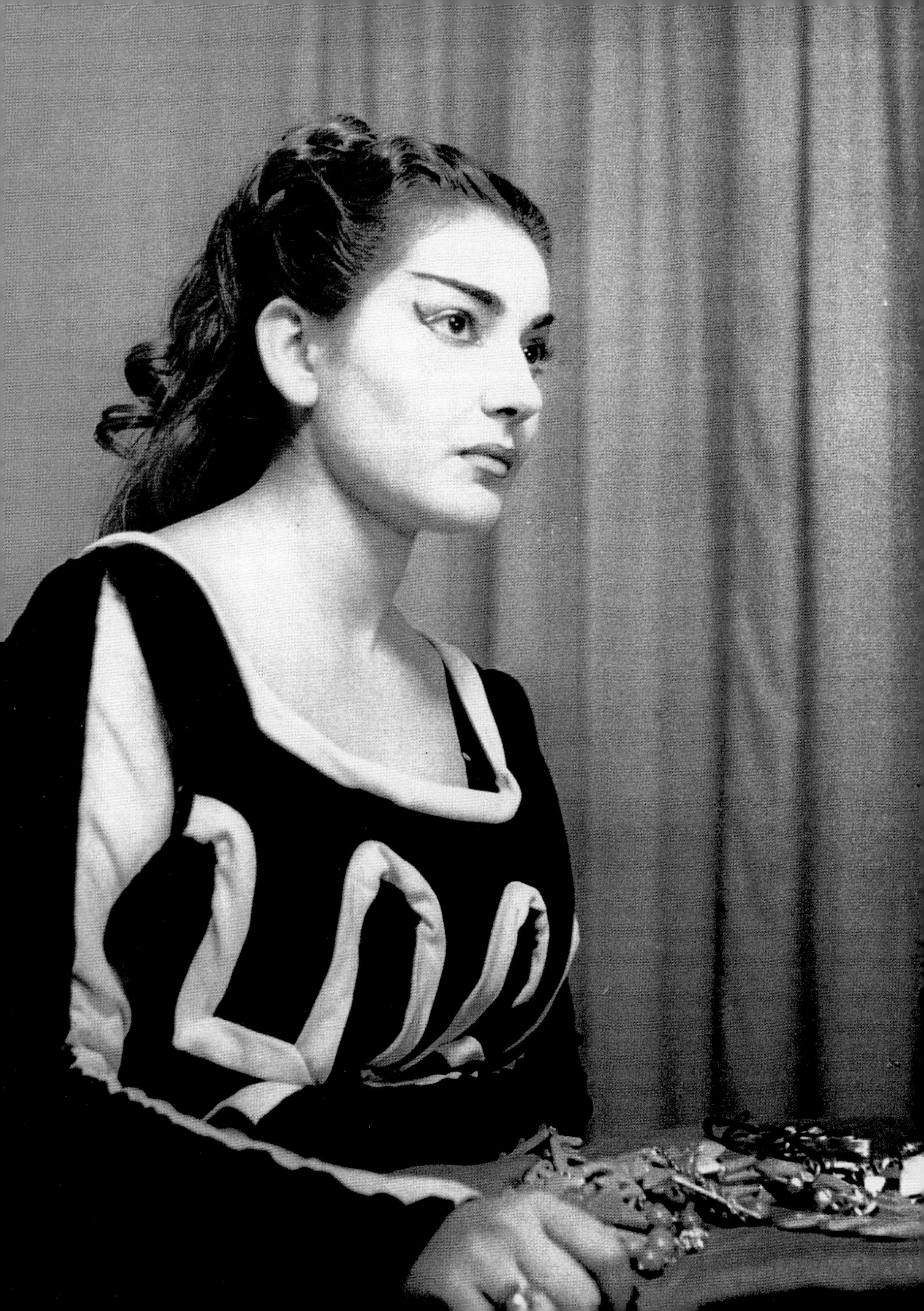

THE BIRTH OF A LEGEND

"Divina!" That howl, with the last vowel prolonged according to the lung capacity of the howler, always comes from above, from those galleries that in the fifties still historically functioned as judge and jury for singers and opera conductors. And that howl, which is peremptory in a way that brooks no appeal, but yet contains a strange note of confusion that turns it into an invocation – that howl begins to be heard always and only when Callas is singing.

When was it heard for the first time? Who can say? And did it happen at La Scala or in Florence? Was it after a *Lucia* or a *Medea*? But it is heard always and only for Callas. A howl that is a coronation and a sudden recognition that Callas inhabits a sphere inaccessible to others, that she is clearly a vocal phenomenon, an incomparable artistic personality. And to reach this point did not, all in all, take her a very long time.

When she sang even people of the profession, like me, got goose-flesh. Her voice was composed of three colors and in passing from one to the other, one could hear the seams. But her virtuosity was such that everything was freed in a vocal expression and musicality that had never before been heard.
GIULIETTA SIMIONATO

Already between 1949 and the early fifties, the artistic profile of Maria Callas is not comparable to that of any living singer. The turning point was reached in January 1949 – thus after only two years of singing in Italy – when within three days Maria went from Wagner's Brunnhilde to Elvira in *Puritani* to substitute at the last moment for an indisposed colleague: two antithetical worlds, two tessituras poles apart, two entirely incompatible vocal exigencies.

As if a weightlifter were to try horse jumping or a javelin thrower to do gymnastic exercises. And in so doing, she cancelled in one blow all the traditional divisions separating the various vocal categories: on the one hand, those who sing Wagner, the *verismo* repertoire, perhaps late Verdi and the "big" Puccini roles like Turandot – in general roles that demand a vocal heavyweight; the in-between voices that sing lyric soprano ranging from "spinto" or dramatic tendencies to *lirico leggero* (never both at once!); and the other extreme, those twittering dolls, the coloratura sopranos, at that time prevalently reduced to being mechanical music boxes specialized in emitting tightrope acrobatics at wild speeds in a stratospheric range.

And here is Callas confronting those acrobatics (to which de Hidalgo had accustomed her) with an immense, dark voice and filling those soprano hyper-spaces with a dense, bronze timbre, an amazing volume and a penetration that was unimaginable in that repertory. This undertaking – for that moment episodic and restricted, by and large, to the ears of theater directors, critics and operatic troupes – would in effect open the way to a whole new

Elvira and Lady Macbeth, two antithetical roles for a voice that could do anything.

direction in the Callas career and, historically speaking, represent the beginning of a revolution that would change the face of Italian opera.

For the moment, however, Maria – who had sung her first *Norma* a few months before the *Die Walküre-Puritani* exploit – begins widening her range of action on various fronts. She continues singing *Tristan* and *Turandot* along with an *Aida* much admired for its display of vocal opulence and variegated shadings; but already between October 1950 and January 1951, she transforms herself into a Rossini soprano with a *Turco in Italia* of soft and brilliant vocalization.

And then, after a *Parsifal* sung for the radio, she faces her first *Traviata* in Florence. In concert she goes even farther, venturing into arias from *Lakmé* or *Dinorah* which had until then been the preserve of the most acrobatic coloraturas and which she alternates with decidedly dramatic pages of Verdi and von Weber. Such things obviously do not go unnoticed. In fact, just about everyone wants her and La Scala – after she had substituted for an ailing Tebaldi in three performances of *Aida* there during April 1950 – offers her the opening of the 1951-52 season in *I Vespri Siciliani*, which she has just sung in Florence at the Maggio Musicale.

They also offer her *Norma* and *The Abduction from the Seraglio* in the subsequent months. But La Scala is still far from being "her" theater. In the hearts of the Milanese box-holders the golden voice of Renata Tebaldi is still firmly anchored. And then, as we have seen, the intrinsic qualities of the Callas voice are still under discussion – and how they are!

Not beautiful, is what is said, in essence, and even decidedly ugly, say her detractors who, with the mark of unrelenting opposition are already beginning to line up and be counted. Suggestive, special, with a harshness and veiled sound that make her modern and expressive, say the more hip critics; imperfectly managed, oddly welded registers, reply the champions of traditional beauty – so very oddly welded in the various registers, in fact, that every now and then something breaks, producing ventriloquist notes in the low register and occasional but spectacular cracking on the top notes.

All true. But at the same time there is the implicit admission that the Callas voice is in fact three voices: the bottom has the color and volume of a mezzo soprano; in the middle, a richness and expansion that you do not find every day; while the top extension is decidedly marvelous. Irregularities, imperfections in such an exceptional organ? Of course. But this is to reckon without the perfection mania of this girl who can hardly see, and whom one can hardly bear to look at, unless she is well made-up and painstakingly dressed, but who, in singing, in study, has found a reason for living and, in ambition, a strong impulse for personal vindication. And Callas studies, stubbornly, to discipline and control her voice, smooth the harshness, fill in the cracks, to acquire the homogeneous quality that nature has not bestowed on her. And all of this, possibly, without detracting from the surplus of raw material that sets her apart. Little by little, the results begin to show.

They are noticed at the Florence Maggio Musicale in 1952 where she is heard as the lead in Rossini's *Armida*. In reality, what is put on the stage is more than anything else a selection from the Pesaro composer's unsingable opera seria (at the sixth degree of difficulty). To manage to mount it at all required such cutting down of the tenor parts that today when there is a full revival of Rossini's singing practices – among the male singers too – when we now hear the recording of that performance it strikes us as a pioneering effort.

But right in the midst of it, at the center of an evening that became legendary thanks to Maria alone – to the point that it became the official date for the start of that Rossini renaissance which in truth only took place quite a few years later – there is a Callas like none that perhaps had ever been heard before, the protagonist of one of the most sensational performances of a purely vocal order that still exists in recording today. Astonishing fireworks, where a penetrating and sulfurous voice launches into the most fantastical ornamentations, then delves into sweet pianissimos unthinkable in a voice of such dimensions, only to rocket into stratospheric high notes that touch high F.

With exploits of this kind, Maria Callas begins to create for herself a legend that we can summarize in the following points:

The voice is an instrument of expression. Notes are not enough, but colors. One paints with one's voice, it must also be acid at times, I need all the colors to express all the feelings.

> *Her appearance revitalized two things, first of all the repertory. An entire category of opera that until then had been considered dead or not performable, she again made possible. And I mean a whole category of opera, not just the ones she sang in. And second, she renewed our way of listening to opera, our demands and thus also the means of satisfying them, which is to say the interpreters. This is the historical Callas. That established, anyone who likes is free to prefer the legendary one.*
> FEDELE D'AMICO

international press coverage; unconditional approval of the majority of the music critics galvanized by the uncommon event; instant hysteria from the greater part of the public, aware of witnessing larger-than-life vocal phenomena; equally instantaneous rejection by another part of the public who see in such delirium a threat to their own preferred singers (generally Tebaldi fans); extreme curiosity on the part of orchestra conductors and theater managers; great diffidence from some colleagues (usually tenors) who fear for their own success in the face of the developing "phenomenon".

Maria will not be long in furnishing further reasons for worry or exaltation in her listeners: within two months, between Mexico City and the Arena of Verona, she sings the light and super-light roles (*Traviata*, *Puritani*, *Lucia* and *Rigoletto*), then the heavyweights (*Tosca*, *Gioconda*). Then she opens the La Scala season for the second year running and her performance of Verdi's Lady Macbeth becomes the point of reference for any subsequent performances (even until today). It all is beginning to be a bit much for many people. The dissenting party took on substance: for them, that Greek woman's voice was by now unquestionably ugly along with the fact that fat and big-nosed as she was, it was impossible to look at her. And then she was unpleasant, presumptuous, arrogant.

During these first very few years of her rise to the top, rumors were circled of a "nasty" Callas which became full blown in later years. On December 7, 1953 Renata Tebaldi opened the La Scala season with Callas applauding her in the audience – a pretense, everyone claimed – the mischievous woman's real intention was just to make her rival nervous. That same year, Maria sings a new addition to her repertory

When she was already singing Lucia, Maria kept strong roles such as Gioconda in her repertoire.

The Birth of a Legend

I do not love extremes even if destiny puts me in extreme situations.

in Florence and later La Scala, another role that would become definitively associated with her name: Medea in Cheubini's opera of that name, one of those roles that seem made to order for all the unusual qualities of her voice, her phrasing, in short, the art of this strange woman who at times seems as possessed as a witch and as apocalyptic as a maenad.

Armida, Lady Macbeth, Medea: roles that gave Callas a special status in which the magical-demonic element played a primary role, making it easy for the listener to identify the role with the interpreter as well as quite particular states of attention and participation.

By now Maria Callas is incontestably a singer *sui generis*, unclassifiable, unique. La Scala gives her roles which could also be sung by others (*Gioconda*, *Trovatore*). But already they are beginning to plan exceptional things for her. Callas is aware of it, she knows she is about to reach the top, and prepares to play her final card. Is she unsightly, actually deformed as her "enemies" say? Very well. In a few months she sheds about forty-five pounds and very soon another twenty. She becomes a new woman. Her fantastic eyes stand out enormous against her pale face with its marked cheekbones. (Only one year earlier, her cheeks were fat to the bursting point.) Her arms and hands are finally free to trace arabesques and to flash out imperiously at the tensest moments; her whirling cloaks create an altogether different effect.

The weight loss is so impressive that the magazines go wild. We have to remember how attentively, at the time, these big social events were covered, events such as the opening of La Scala and other important theaters, which were occasions for

Maria and the "great fathers": Toscanini, De Sabata and (with his back to the camera) Antonino Votto.

Maria Callas raises her arms, she unwinds: now she is no longer the hoopoe symbolized by the proud, tawny crest and the sharp beak, rusty as though it had been steeped in a wound, but she is one of those Cretan women who brandished serpents, but as livid themselves as deadly serpents.
MARIO PRAZ

demonstrating to post-war Italy the standards of class and elegance which had to be totally reinvented. What had Callas done? How had she managed it? Thanks to her vanished weight, Maria Callas escapes from the music columns to appear on other pages inside the papers and conquer publications that earlier had never shown any interest in her, except perhaps in passing.

I don't know exactly what happened. I ate a lot of fruit, meat and greens, but I didn't take anything, absolutely nothing. I never take as much as an aspirin. Good heavens, if I knew a system for losing weight, I wouldn't keep it a secret. I could become the richest woman in the world.

The so-called women's press now seems unable to do without this story of a modern metamorphosis and ventures into the most fantastic inventions – among them, the one given great credence about her going so far as to have swallowed a voracious parasite. However all that may be, the fact that an opera star's weight loss, drastic as it might be, becomes, in 1953-1954 a veritable journalistic event, shows that something was in the air favorable to the attention given by the media to someone like Maria Callas.

And Callas, among other things, has the nerve, four days after the last performance of *Medea*, to win another legendary La Scala triumph in *Lucia di Lammermoor* conducted by Karajan. It is January 1954, and if she is not yet as emaciated as she will be in December, she is still thin enough to be able to confront the "mad scene" in a spotlight on a dark stage, her loose hair falling onto a white pleated gown and the staging concentrated on her face and the play of her speaking hands. Hers is a Lucia already tried out in many other theaters, successfully recorded and totally new in its dark, painful, unbridled romantic concept. A Lucia madly in love, true, but who makes the madness felt as an extreme torment of the soul, a truly

Norma, one of the key roles in the Callas legend.

> *Above and beyond the polish of her portamentos and filigree, the tastefulness of her colors and her very vivid trill, there was the conviction she created in the listener that those mechanical ingredients, however refined, meant nothing in themselves and that overcoming them was precisely what counted: getting out of the workshop, that is, and flying in the poetic heavens.*
> EUGENIO GARA

lacerated mind. A modern, psychoanalytic Lucia that will exalt her admirers, now ever more numerous.

Even if her detractors do not loosen their grip, the large mass of her adorers (and the word is *not* excessive as the chronicles show) seem to have burned their bridges and gone over to sheer fanaticism. "Divina!" is precisely the howl-invocation which, as we have seen, begins to fall from above on certain of her evenings. To this, the true Callas fanatic adds all the characteristics of the fan (diffused hysteria, uncontrolled enthusiasm, personal idolatry, showers of flowers, souvenir collecting, the taste for self-sacrifice in accepting all manner of discomfort for the sake of hearing the idol sing whenever possible) exasperated by the absolute conviction of Callas's supremacy over all other singers and its corollary: the clear sense of irritation in hearing any of the others.

This, of course, is hardly the attitude suited to pacifying spirits, even less so when the highest officials of a theater (La Scala, for instance) begin to openly favor one singer (Maria) over others (Tebaldi, for instance). It is just this rivalry with Tebaldi, at around the mid-fifties, which transcends the limits of the world of opera to take on the character of a public nature and an affair of state.

Obviously the basic motive of conflict is supremacy at La Scala where both aim to reign as uncontested queen for questions of principle, prestige – today we would call it "image". This was still an epoch when the Milanese opera house could boast of an effective world primacy and when being number one in the hall of Piermarini really meant something. Obviously too, the press was not going to be content with a merely strategic war between the two prima donnas but was hard at work creating two highly colorful personages: on the one hand, the Angel, and on the other, the Devil; *here* Italy, and *there* the rest of the world, and so on as the embroidering continued.

> *Tebaldi has one defect, she has no backbone.*
> MARIA
> *Maybe so, but I have one thing she hasn't got, and that's heart.*
> RENATA

Not that they had to look far for the colorful. Quite the contrary. Here is Renata: *Italianissima* by birth and standards, much attached to her mother (who follows her everywhere to the point of waiting in the wings when she sings), with a pleasant nature and proven gentleness, ideal in the roles of simple and good heroines (Desdemona, Mimi) and above all, endowed with a voice of exceptional beauty. A natural, luxurious voice, very rich in color, large, flexible with a timbre that finds very few points of comparison in the entire century: the voice of an angel, as Toscanini seems to have said, and which everyone recognizes.

And over there, Maria, quite the contrary:

*Compare myself with Tebaldi?
It would be like comparing
champagne with cognac – no, better,
champagne with Coca-Cola.*
MARIA

*If it is true that Callas's voice is like
champagne, it is also true that
champagne quickly turns to vinegar.*
RENATA

An already memorable interpretation waiting for the final touches of a directorial genius.

Greek-American-Italian (and for some, with the demerit of being a foreigner...), with awful relations with her mother and sister, a prickly disposition, tending to very undiplomatic fits of rage, specialized in the roles of "dark" ladies (Medea, Lady Macbeth) and unquestionably equipped with a highly unorthodox voice capable of infinite shadings, true, but by dint of unceasing work. And "beautiful" – as many never tire of repeating – you certainly cannot call it.

In a situation of this kind, what need is there to invent? Thus the pairing Callas-Tebaldi becomes indivisible and any pretext will do for publishing photos, press releases, declarations and provocative acts... Maria, for example, often goes to hear Tebaldi and sits conspicuously in a box to make her nervous – especially when she pretends to applaud, but it is clear that her clapping hands do not touch. Renata, like the nice girl she is, replies on the level of her generosity, her philanthropy, because it is well known that Maria is quite tight-fisted. And so it goes, to the delight, all in all, of the rival camps.

On the artistic level, however, there is much more at stake, above all from a historical perspective. The two contenders have only two important things in common: each records regularly for their own label, under exclusive contract – Decca for Renata, EMI for Maria, and frequently they record the same works in competition and at the same time, sometimes in the same year, from *La Traviata* to *Tosca*, and *Madam Butterfly*, *Aida*, *La Forza del Destino*, *Trovatore*, *Cavalleria Rusticana*, *Manon Lescaut* – and each sings in fixed tandem with a tenor: Mario Del Monaco with Renata, Giuseppe Di Stefano with Maria.

They differ in everything else, however, and this will become even more pronounced in the future. Maria sings the early nineteenth-century repertoire, climaxing in Bellini and Donizetti; wins her most acclaimed victories in operas forgotten or very rarely performed (*Medea, Armida, Anna Bolena, Il Pirata, Poliuto*); and already mixes genres, styles and tessituras. Renata, after an early period in which she did not lack for rare and stimulating works (*The Siege of Corinth, Fernando Cortez, Olimpia* and Verdi's *Giovanna d'Arco*), opts for the serene traditional path of late Verdi, Puccini and an occasional work of the *Giovane Scuola*, incessantly repeating her most tried and true

The Birth of Legend

> *Maria Callas was for singing what Toscanini was for conducting.*
> RICCARDO MUTI

> *For all those who sing, Callas is the goddess who once and for all blended words and music.*
> LUCIANO PAVAROTTI

roles without once changing or taking a risk.

Thus the lack of novelties penalizes Tebaldi as well as the fact that she has not found a director of genius who can make a "modern" singer of her by transforming her face, figure and gesture and imbuing her with charisma. If Maria represents the new path, Renata is the faithful guardian of tradition. Two different roads, two dissimilar figures without any real points of contact nor of friction except for the circumscribed dominion of a fief – La Scala – which Maria will conquer without half trying. There were simply too many operatic roles which could be entrusted to her.

After *Lucia* in April 1954, she is heard there in *Alceste* and *Don Carlo* – she is heard *and* seen, because now she is distinctly beautiful, statuesque and imperious with that engrossed face and those eyes – eyes which capture directors and spectators. Incomparable is the intellectual curiosity she arouses and the aura of the socialite diva which begins to surround her. Renata (who, in another repertory, may have sung just as many operas as her rival) feels not unjustifiably neglected. She goes to the Metropolitan Opera in New York where she instantly becomes one of the most beloved of prima donnas. Maria reigns alone at La Scala. She owes it primarily to herself, but she gets incomparable help from a director of genius: Luchino Visconti.

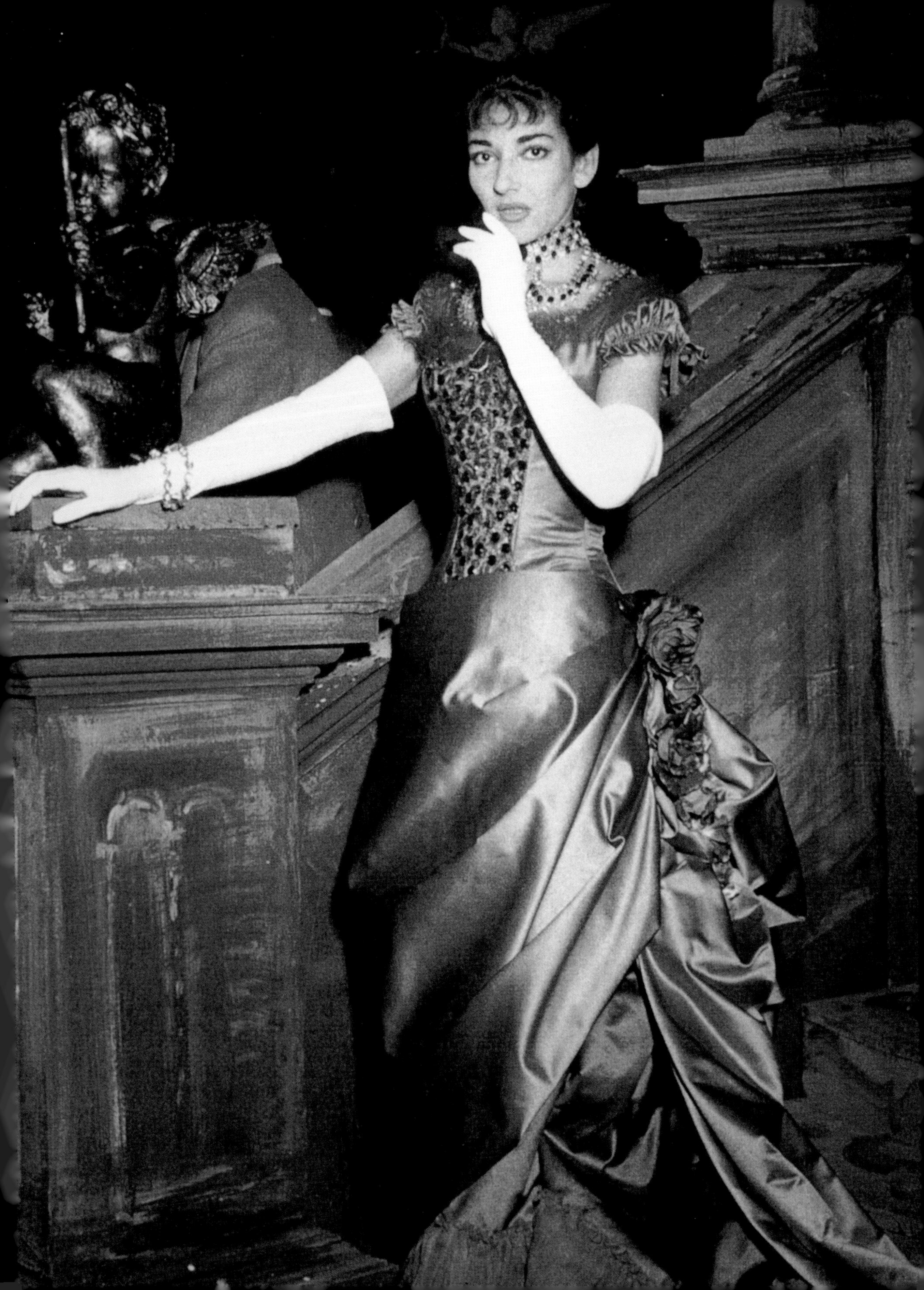

CALLAS-VISCONTI

In 1953 Luchino Visconti, along with Giorgio Strehler, is the new man of the Italian theater. The convinced champion of a "director's theater", in full opposition to a kind of theater where everything is subordinate to the leading actor or actress. He enjoyed solid popularity in the immediate post-war years and had presented shows of great impact due to his choice of texts as well as originality of staging.

He had specialized in two categories: on the one hand, highly pertinent contemporary plays (Cocteau's *Les parents terribles*, Sartre's *Huis clos*, Achard's *Adam*, Kirkland's *Tobacco Road*, and above all Arthur Miller's *Death of a Traveling Salesman* and Tennessee Williams' *Glass Menagerie* or *A Streetcar Named Desire*). Thanks to such plays, themes like incest, male and female homosexuality, infanticide, poverty, alcoholism and nymphomania also erupted onto Italian stages, often arousing scandal in the public and the press, in scabrous stagings of an exasperated realism.

On the other hand, he had produced the great classics of the past (Shakespeare's *Troilus and Cressida* and *As You Like It*, or Alfieri's *Oreste*), staged in a sensationally opulent Baroque style and the most fantastic figurative exuberance. His mania for detail was legendary, as were his taste for a kind of recitation that left nothing to chance, and his capacity to get the most out of actresses with strong personalities. Under his direction, leading ladies like Sarah Ferrati and Rina Morelli won laurels on an international level, while disquieting modern masques, such as Paolo Stoppa's, affirmed their place, and painters like Salvador Dali liberated their visionary talents.

In the realm of cinema too, Luchino Visconti's work had made history with recognized masterpieces such as *Ossessione*, *La terra trema* and *Bellissima*. His rich historical fresco *Senso* had just been presented, a film in which for the first time on the screen he expressed his fantastic taste for decor, for the richest figurative splendor, and for extensive references to music, literature, painting, architecture and furnishings. Furthermore, Visconti as a personality was made-to-order to attract the attention of what was not yet known as the media: Duke Visconti of Modrone, the descendant of a family that had determined the destiny of Milan for centuries, aristocratic to the tips of his toes but known for Communist leanings.

Very rich and imperious, surrounded by a

I have worked for years and years with stage actors, film actors, ballet dancers, singers and I must say that Maria was perhaps the most disciplined person whom I ever ran across. Not only does she not ask for fewer rehearsals, she wants more and she participates until the last minute with the same intensity, giving everything she has, always singing with her full voice.

LUCHINO VISCONTI

Maria's new look: lovely, elegant and with her famous jewels.

court of very handsome men and women of mind-boggling charisma, "scandalously" homosexual, Luchino Visconti set standards for the world of Italian theater/cinema so high as to influence indelibly the whole culture of the second half of the nineteenth century.

In 1954 he has as yet to set his seal on his beloved world of opera – a world that he has known intimately ever since he was a child in the family box at La Scala, the theatrical symbol of Milan in which his grandfather was a stockholder. This world, more than any other at the time, needed the kind of cleaning up and reinterpretation in a modern key that had marked Visconti's work in the prose theater for the past eight years.

To do this, by his own admission, Visconti needed a unique prima donna, a creature with whom and on whom to model a new style and set new standards. He needed a singer with the imperiousness, the sculpted accents and the modern disquietude of a Ferrati, the dreamy sweetness that yet was ready to become a fluttering wing of madness of a Morelli.

That singer, that prima donna was Maria.

Maria was a marvel. I admired her for years, ever since she had sung Norma and Kundry in Rome. Each time she sang, I reserved the same box and when she came out for curtain calls I shouted like mad. I sent her flowers and in the end we met. She was fat, but on stage she was superb. She was already remarkable, her gestures inspired us. Where had she learned them? She had done it all by herself.
LUCHINO VISCONTI

Visconti already knew her, had heard her several times in Rome, remembered her as Wagner's Kundry and Rossini's Fiorilla, totally dissimilar in character and vocal category, and so perfect to show vocal flexibility and variety of phrasing, interpretative talent and capacity for transformation.

Their first encounter was fated to be at the top: the revival of an almost entirely forgotten opera, Spontini's *La Vestale* for the 1954 opening of the La Scala season, which is to say for the most important operatic date in Italy. As we have seen, Maria was someone entirely different from what Visconti remembered: very thin, sculptured looking, and even blonde, no less. Furthermore her morale was at its peak this season, holding as she did a contract for five different operas in comparison to Tebaldi's single role in *La Forza del Destino*. And of these five, one was a season opener, three were new productions for her, and three with Visconti as stage director. What more could she ask for? Thus her state of mind was in general excellent, she was more receptive to others, and her desire for perfection as voracious as ever.

As for her professional qualities, they were recognized by all as being one of her strong points and it was impossible that this should fail to win over a workaholic and maniac for detail like Visconti. Maria saw in him the man who had everything she lacked (birth, rank, culture, refinement, incomparable taste) and perhaps she intuited that with his help she could elevate all her natural qualities (nobility of gesture and comportment, archaic culture of whose magnitude she was probably only instinctively aware for now). Visconti seized on her mania for perfection and her desire to transform herself as well, of course, on her immense artistic gift which already at that time set her apart.

Theirs was the encounter of two giants mutually fascinated with each other who met on the hard, obstinate terrain of daily work. She would come out of the experience definitively, irreversibly transformed, while he would gain professional luster and prestige and become in this field too a point of reference for his and all future time.

For the moment they study and discover each other on a terrain that is atypical for both when all is said and done. Spontini's *La Vestale* commits them to a rather restricted

With her beloved friend Giulietta Simionato after the triumph of Anna Bolena.

We chose poses inspired by the great classical French tragic actresses or by Greek tragedy. Because this is the kind of actress Maria must be: classical.
LUCHINO VISCONTI,
SPEAKING OF *LA VESTALE*

neo-classical musical and figurative language. He creates fascinating *tableaux vivants* while she watches over word and gesture.

To enliven what could easily become a little "wooden", he gives the tenor Franco Corelli a costume-movie tunic to wear that leaves his Olympian legs bare (and which will win him the nickname "Cosciadoro", or "Golden Thighs," forever after). For her part, she adds a high C to the second act aria which, at the end of a vortex of vehement phrases, gives the audience a shot of *Medea*-like adrenaline and ensures her an ovation.

But the couple's first true triumph will come three months later on March 5, 1955 with Bellini's *La Sonnambula*. In between, Maria accepts to sing a *Chenier*, at La Scala again, in substitution for a *Trovatore* that was planned. She then went to Rome for a *Medea*, and fortunately, had thirty days of rehearsals before confronting the Bellini score.

For any opera addict, the idea of a singer going from the *verismo* accents of Maddalena di Coigny to the vertiginous flights of *Medea* – which, furthermore, are based on a very low tessitura bordering on a mezzo soprano register – and finally to venture into Amina's stratospheric top range, means only one thing: that voice is on the fast road to ruin. And so it was, in fact, to be, but no one had as yet noticed, least of all Maria herself who was making a habit of such madness, but who would soon have to consider being more prudent.

In any case, thirty days of rehearsal for a repertory opera – really a routine work – like

A theatrical look with splendid evening gowns designed for her by Biki.

> *With that long neck, the streamlined body, those arms, those fingers, Maria had a way of being that was uniquely hers. No one will ever be able to imitate her.*
> LUCHINO VISCONTI

La Sonnambula are an indication that something unusual was going on. And, in fact, Visconti gave birth to a show that made history and added one more event to La Scala's post-war legend. For, determined to recreate the romantic world of Théophile Gautier and revive the myth of the nineteenth-century ballerina, Visconti combines *The Specter of the Rose*, the epitome of "white" ballets with Carla Fracci in the leading role.

And it is on none other than Fracci that he models Maria: costume, make-up, hair-do, steps and gestures – everything. Because Maria, turned brunette again, is so thin by now that she can even dare to do this. Visconti has her move on the stage with her eyes shut during a sleep-walking scene guided by the scent of a light perfume. He manages her arm movements which are like beating wings so that for her and with her he revives the ghosts of Grisi, Taglioni and Cerrito.

Did Maria know who they were? Probably not. But this too is what she wants from men like Visconti: to learn, absorb, know, after which she develops it all in her own way guided by an instinct that borders on witchcraft. Visconti creates a world around her, but for her to bring that world to life, an accent, a word suffices. The voice of Medea becomes airy and transparent, connecting strings of variations with her habitual fluency, but now with a homogeneity of registers that must have cost her infinite labor but which sounds entirely natural.

Visconti's finale of *La Sonnambula* is a stroke of genius, an act of homage to Maria and her coronation. Luchino asks her to abandon the role of Amina and sing the final rondo in front of the footlights, all alone in a ballerina's white costume to which he has added a fantastic prima donna's necklace. And while she is flying through the final variations in a palpable state of vocal grace (to which the live recording bears witness), he has all the lights in the house turned on, bringing the audience to such a condition of exasperated excitement that the screams begin even before the end of the rondo so

that Maria's final top note not only has to soar above orchestra and chorus, but also above the tumult in the theater. It is a total triumph, Maria has been crowned in public and nothing and no one can challenge her supremacy at La Scala. Who can stop her?

During the performances of *La Sonnambula*, she rehearses the part of Fiorilla with Zeffirelli in *Il Turco in Italia*, one of her three Rossini roles. (Only three? It is better to refrain from thinking of what, after *Armida*, a voice like hers could have made of *Ermione*, *Elisabetta Regina d'Inghilterra*, or *Semiramide*, if the time had been ripe for a correct execution of the "serious" Rossini repertoire.) In the role of a woman thirsting for life and encumbered with an older, clearly inadequate husband, who can tell if she had not begun to realize some parallels with her own private life... What is certain is that her Fiorilla, very worldly and amused (yet with that "seriousness" at bottom which is Maria's hallmark), a viper and a shrew when it is useful, suits her down to the ground and she has a lot of fun with it.

It is equally certain that the rhythm of Callas's life had taken on the cadences of an upper-middle-class Milanese lady's. Her house in Via Buonarroti is elegant and splendid with its Renaissance paintings and decor, choice antiques and professional touches (Visconti will not have denied her his advice). Her wardrobe is entirely entrusted to Biki who dresses all of the right Milanese ladies. She moves in tony circles: not only do the most prestigious salons fight over her presence, but a true court of adoring

---

She walked on padded feet like a tiger. Her gestures were broad and theatrical almost as if she were about to fling a shawl, a veil, the edge of a cape over her shoulder.

BIKI

Pygmalion and Galatea after La Vestale *and* Ifigenia, *the first and last of their happy collaborations.*

admirers surrounds her which comprises the aristocracy and the high society of industrialists, artists, men of letters (let us not forget that many of the most important intellectuals of the time write about her, which is something unique).

Although her faithful consort is always by her side (he who is so little interested in society and social standing), Luchino continues to be her main point of reference. Now, in three weeks time, he is making to measure for her that which for many remains the quintessential Callas production: the Visconti *Traviata*. Maria has sung it often and has even recorded it. But now she studies it as if for the first time.

He has very precise ideas about it and asks her to recreate two of the greatest interpreters of the Dumas piece from which Verdi took his masterpiece: Eleonora Duse (whose black costume he has copied for Maria in the first act) and Sarah Bernhardt. He draws on his vast culture for references and quotations, suggesting to Maria a gesture here, a glance there. She assimilates and works it out, quoting and at the same time creating. It is here that her psychological dependence on Visconti

> *I always put limits on her and objectives. Then I told her: within these limits do whatever you like. This is only possible with an artist whom you trust completely because you know her feeling for* tempo, *her musical instinct as a dramatic and tragic actress.*
> LUCHINO VISCONTI

reaches its acme. Was she in love with him as many claim? Perhaps. Many women fall in love with declared homosexuals and in Visconti's life it will become a common occurrence. Certain is that she seeks him out, demands his constant presence in the wings, and – it appears – is openly jealous about him.

She knows, naturally, that she owes much to him, but perhaps what she primarily sees in him is one of the rare "elect" who in his own way is able to reach her own heights. Their collaboration in *Traviata* is admirable and very close. The fanatical attention to every gesture, every pose is even, some think, responsible for depriving Maria's singing of some of its spontaneity. And it is true that among her recordings there are other versions which on the vocal and expressive levels are more riveting, with more clearly worked out accentuation and more lacerating emotion.

This La Scala Violetta – conducted by Carlo Maria Giulini, staged with tasteful luxury and with Lila De Nobili's sets and costumes in equally incomparable taste – remains a unique Callas/Violetta for its fusion of word and gesture, music and movement. A "naturalistic" Violetta, as has been said, that never loses sight of the true story – in effect, sordid and miserable enough – of Alphonsine Plessis, a prostitute who died at the age of twenty-three of consumption. A story, however, that first passes through the filtering hands of not only Dumas and Verdi, but also, as we have seen, of several interpreters (and in the impressive final scene as she lies back with wide-open eyes, Maria will recall Garbo's Margherita Gautier too).

Between rehearsals and performances, Maria and Luchino are inseparable. By now Visconti is not merely the man who creates unforgettable productions for Callas, who refines her miming and gestures to a perfection, beyond all others. His influence also extends off-stage with valuable advice about interior decoration, as we have noted, as well as careful supervision of what later became known as her "look" combined with cultural stimulus to which Maria was far from insensitive.

During these months Maria adds to her musical supremacy not only an enviable social status, but also, for an opera singer, a most uncommon attention on the part of the media. The women's and fashion magazines fight over her, photo reports cover her visits to Biki's salon, do stories about her in the theater, at home and out walking. Now she

> *On stage I have always tried to find intensity, essentiality. A pointless gesture is a foolish gesture.*

The creative team of La Sonnambula.

A symbolic image of the new direction: Maria in La Vestale *directed by Visconti.*

gets a whim to imitate Audrey Hepburn's look in *Roman Holiday*, which she admired so very much. For the fat and clumsy Maria of just a few years earlier, it is no small accomplishment.

Meanwhile, the success of *Traviata* is such that the production is put back on the boards in the following season for fifteen performances. Not only that, but it will turn out to be a stumbling block for future attempts to stage the opera at La Scala. Naturally enough, no one will sing the part in this production after Maria, but it will actually create a kind of malediction on the work at the Milan theater for almost forty years.

The new production in 1964, for example, was withdrawn after only three performances, despite the prestigious names of Karajan and Zeffirelli, when Mirella Freni and Anna Moffo (who replaced her after the tempestuous first night) were called to summary justice by the public. Then total silence until 1992, when none other than Riccardo Muti used all of his prestige, insisted on presenting the production with a cast of debutantes, just to pre-empt the danger of uncomfortable comparisons.

But none of the great singers of those decades was able to obtain the blessing of La Scala – and the list includes names such as Renata Scotto, Beverly Sills, Montserrat Caballé and Ileana Cotrubas, all very different from each other and all very different from Callas, but all worthy of being heard in the role. For the rest, the hysteria of the so-called "Callas widows" – those gallery goers who, having lost their idol, decided to make war on any other singer who dared to take on her roles in the Piermarini hall – afflicted La Scala's opening nights for years with demonstrations where theatrics, ignorance and provincialism ended by doing a disservice to the very idol they claimed to be "protecting".

To meet up with Visconti again, Maria would have to wait until April 1957 when, after a revival of their *Sonnambula*, Luchino led her to one more triumph of the kind that even today remains one of the pillars of the Callas temple. He, who had just put his seal on *The Death of a Salesman*, one of the greatest successes of the Morelli-Stoppa team (in whose company Marcello Mastroianni also shines), this time guided her through the England of Henry VIII in Donizetti's *Anna Bolena*. This too a forgotten opera, this too, a posteriori, the birth of a revival: the revival of Donizetti, just as *Armida* marked the revival of Rossini.

The point of reference, obligatory in this case: the paintings of Holbein. And with the complicity of Nicola Benois' sets and costumes, Visconti created the halls and stairways, the parks and towers of a gloomy and menacing England. He masterfully regulated the movements of crowds, cutting out strongly characterized silhouettes: Nicola Rossi Lemeni's Henry VIII, grim and bejeweled; the incandescent Jane Seymour of Giulietta Simionato in a flaming red dress; and Maria's statuesque Boleyn, at first clothed all in shades of blue, and later, for the ascension to the chopping block, in black with her hair hanging loose.

She, more regal than ever, finds one of her key roles, one of those which permit her to soar through several registers alternating the most piercing melancholy with raging invective, loneliness and public rebellion, until reaching one of those final scenes of which Donizetti possessed the secret. And so now La Scala – which in the meantime had not loved her excessively as Rosina in *The Barber of Seville* and had only given her due in an atypical role as *Fedora* which, however, leaves no opportunity for arousing any great enthusiasm – once again experiences one of those mythical nights which only Callas seems able to create.

From the restless recitative of her entrance, to the sweet delirium of one of Donizetti's most famous "cantilenas", from the prayer to the raging invective of the final cabaletta as the queen ascends to the chopping block, forgiving and cursing at the same time, Maria's tour de force is one of those that is destined to become legend from the moment in which they first occur. The gallery shouts "divina" and from that finale will begin a wave of Donizetti revivals and it will be the point of reference for all the great interpreters of Maria's generation and the next, from Leyla Gencer to Montserrat Caballé, from Joan Sutherland to Beverly Sills, to mention only the most important ones.

But one score alone will Maria take for her own from the flood of *Lucrezia Borgias*, *Maria Stuardas*, *Roberto Devereuxs*, *Maria di Rohans*, *Belisarios* and *Les Martyres*, up to and including the most unheard of and forgotten titles. Maria will take *Poliuto*. It was to take place on December 7, 1960 and be an addition to the list of her collaborations with Visconti, but it was not to be: in protest against the censorship that interrupted the performances of Testori's *Arialda* that he had staged for the Morelli-Stoppa team and blocked the release of *Rocco and His Brothers* in movie theaters, Visconti retires from the theatrical scene.

Thus his final staging for Maria is Gluck's *Iphigenia in Tauris* which went on one month after the last performance of *Anna Bolena*. A seldom performed, neo-classical work like *La Vestale*, which began their collaboration, it is also the one instance of disagreement between "la divina" and her Pygmalion. He intends it to be a homage to Tiepolo, loads Maria with sensational costumes, yards of satin and cascades of pearls, crescent moons in her hair and poses inspired by the

---

If she had not sung, she would have been an extraordinary actress, above all a great interpreter of classic Greek theater.
IRENE PAPAS

Maria has tragedy in her blood, the tragic pain of Euripedes' characters.
LUCHINO VISCONTI

Venetian frescos in Palazzo Labia. For her part, Iphigenia arouses all her Greek blood – she would have it archaic.

They cannot come to terms and their journey together ends here. Of course, neither of them knows it and in fact Visconti's name is one that most frequently comes up in Maria's plans for always renewed hypotheses of a *Traviata*, for new, bizarre roles which he proposes when her career appears to have reached – and it has – a point of no return: Salome, the Marschallin, Kostelnicka in *Jenufa*…

But even if their collaboration was squeezed into five shows over only two La Scala seasons, it was of historical importance in the world of Italian opera in the twentieth century. Callas-Visconti was and has remained over time an inseparable pairing of names, a symbol of renewal and modernity, the highest degree of perfectionism and quality. With them the concept of director's theater – something entirely new in opera – staked out its place in Italy and from there spread throughout the world.

A way of making theater which inspired first Franco Zeffirelli, Luchino's former assistant, and Giorgio Strehler. In time it became the new reality of the international scene, the unquestioned dogma – possibly the only thing that assured the survival of opera, especially in those periods (and there have been some) when there were no great singing personalities around.

THE WORLD AND ROME

Whereas the years between December 1954 and June 1957 are for Maria primarily the period she works with Visconti, it does not mean that there were no other high points in her career. On the contrary, these are the years in which Maria Callas's vertiginous charisma, amplified by phonograph records and underscored by the media, echoes around the world, creating high anticipation wherever she appears and soon blossoming into the dimension of legend that makes Callas into a living myth – perhaps despite herself – far beyond the milieu in which she moves.

In 1954 Maria strides out with an American debut that will have great repercussions in the future: in seventeen days she sings *Norma*, *Traviata* and *Lucia di Lammermoor* in

Opera is a corpse, which still has a few nervous twitches.

Chicago doing only two performances of each role, but enough to create a certain "Callas fever" in America too which is accentuated the following year in *Puritani*, *Trovatore* and an unexpected *Madam Butterfly*. The American public adores creating idols, and Maria possesses many elements that can excite interest: European origins, a difficult childhood, the unhappy adolescence of an ugly duckling, an oppressive mother and a too-pretty sister, the inimitable talent that

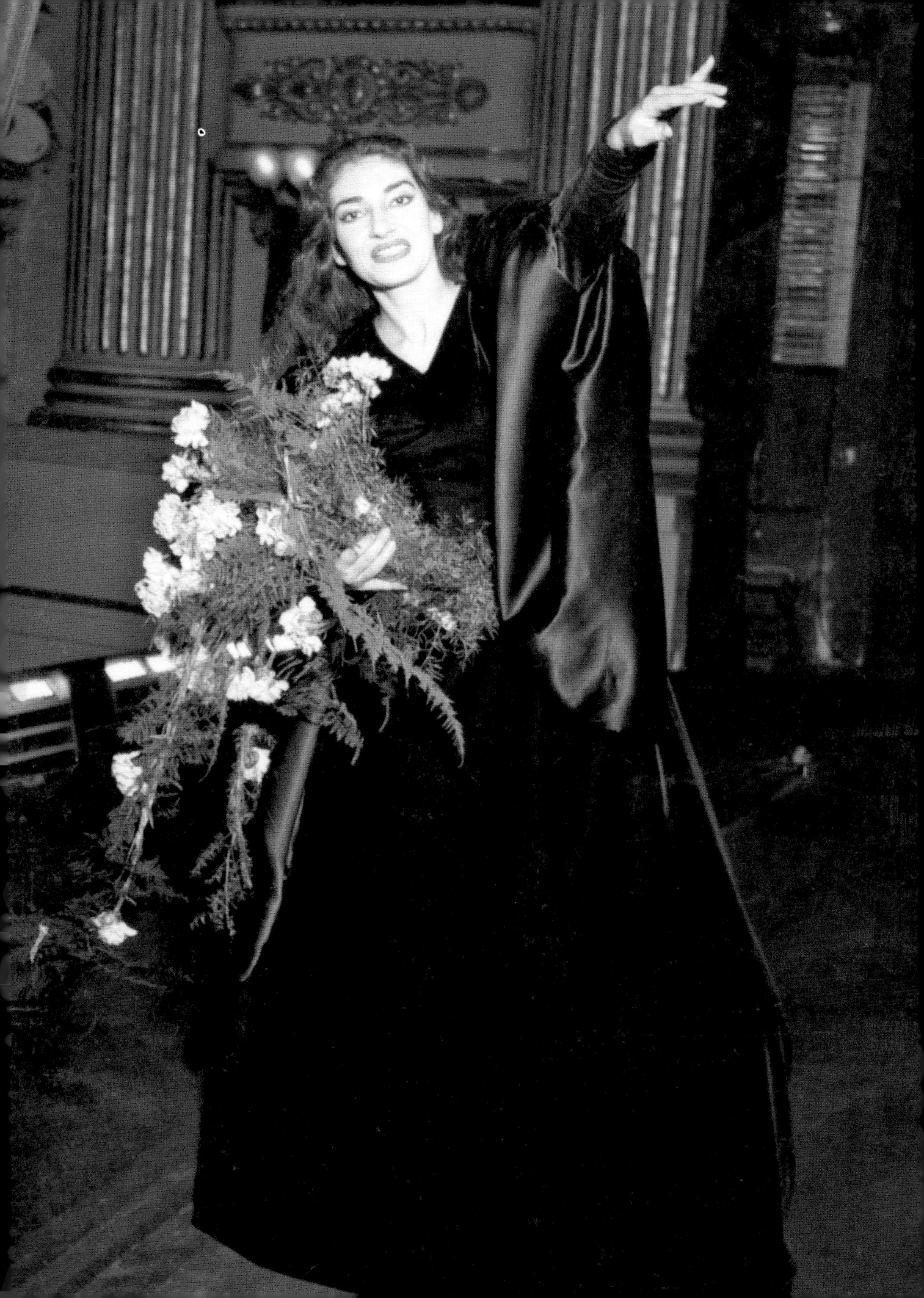

Here and on the next page: Maria's flamboyant gestures during her solo curtain calls soon become a part of the Callas legend.

vindicates her, a sensational plunge in weight (to which a population with serious obesity problems is particularly sensitive), a supposedly difficult character, and the temperament of a tiger…

And so the press begins to pay particular attention to displays of that character and that temperament – little does it matter whether public or private. A legal incident arises regarding a one-time impresario who claims exclusive rights to her and demands a percentage of all her earnings up to that moment. This brings on an overwhelming nervous blow-up in Maria and instantly a photo is circulated worldwide with her eyes looking demonic and her mouth twisted as she spouts invective.

It is only a matter of time before Callas finds photographers on her trail wherever she may go, whatever she may do. Worst of all is that the journalists are on her heels trying to provoke her with questions that are out of place: how long it has been since she has seen her mother; if she knows that Renata Tebaldi has had a triumph in New York; when she will make her debut at the Metropolitan; why she demands to be paid so much more than any of her other colleagues; how she has managed to lose weight in so short a time.

Gossip of no importance, certainly, but having to face this every time she appears anywhere starts wearing down the nerves. However, Maria has learned to use the weapon of diplomacy which is not part of her nature: she smiles, tries to circumvent the booby traps and on one count, at least, has an answer ready: the long awaited Metropolitan Opera debut will take place in October 1956 with *Norma*.

Maria arrives in New York girded with her past triumphs at La Scala, the sensation she has created in Chicago, and the publicity campaign waged by EMI records. Does

> *It was unforgettable when she sang* Casta Diva, *how, with great evocative force she made one feel all the moons of Leopardi: the candid or setting moon of Bruto Minore and Sappho's wandering shepherd...*
> ALBERTO ARBASINO

America love things bigger than life? This then is their woman: has there not been talk everywhere of the delirium her *Lucia* aroused in Berlin and Vienna under Karajan? People waiting in line all night to procure a ticket? A twenty-minute ovation after her "mad scene"?... If Americans are affected by these excesses, the press campaign mounted for Maria is on a Hollywood scale and her debut arouses expectations that go beyond the confines of the Metropolitan and the U.S. musical world.

On October 29, 1956, then, Maria Callas sings for the first time in the most important opera house of the city where she was born. She is not in great form and she does not do her best – a fact which sincerely troubles and pains her – but anyway the thing has been done and the VIP audience gives her due, and all in all her public image comes out strengthened.

Between October 29 and mid-December 1956, Maria sings *Norma*, *Tosca* and *Lucia di Lammermoor* at the Met. That theater serves for her international career and her prestige, but the system established there by Rudolf Bing, an Austrian who runs it in a dictatorial manner, does not please her one little bit. Used as she is by now to having productions mounted for her which have no equal anywhere in the world, with the certitude of having an entire theater staff ready to give her all the support she needs to create "something beautiful", she finds herself having to sing *Lucia* in a twenty-year-old production, extremely overdone, in which others have appeared before her and still others will do so after her.

In comparison to the standard she has by now reached, the "repertory theater" which Bing aims for represents a step backwards. (Are we doing *Tosca* again this season? Very good, the production is ten years old, but still serviceable. So then – three performances for Callas, three for Tebaldi, and three for Milanov. That way no one can complain. And for next year we book that Italian singer who is so well spoken of, we reconfirm Tebaldi and let's see if Callas is willing to take over the role or if she wants to change operas...).

Her relations with the managing director – who nevertheless admires her above all

> *Her debut was without doubt the most exciting of all those which I experienced at the Met during the whole time of my management.*
> RUDOLF BING

Signing autographs in Paris en route for Chicago.

*I am not aggressive by nature.
I am sorry when I have to defend
myself. It is not in me to attack.
Art is never aggressive.*

others – cannot help but be on a collision course. However that may be, her stay in New York – along with excursions to Philadelphia, Washington and, in February, Chicago again – put her into contact with a world of millionaires and magnates which could not help but impress her. And at her side, the horrid Elsa Maxwell makes her first appearance, the devilish columnist of Hedda Hopper's and Louella Parsons' ilk, a professional gossip as ignorant as she is vulgar, detested but revered by all, seeing that one of her articles – and she churns them out daily – can make or break a career.

By now, Callas begins to need someone like Maxwell to defend her against the flood of generally frivolous articles, always misinformed and almost always of a scandal-mongering sort that the popular press is grinding out about her. Callas fights with her colleagues, Callas tells her mother to jump out of a window if she cannot earn a living, Callas risks losing her voice as a result of dieting, Callas bickers with Bing… and moreover: Callas costs too much and the Vienna State Opera renounces its projects with her (true), Callas cancels a performance (it can happen to anyone, but in her case, though, it makes headlines).

Understandably, Maria's nerves begin to give way, while physical fatigue does the rest and the heedless alternating of roles and tessituras gives her the knockout punch. In July 1957, three days after the last performance of an admirable *Sonnambula* in Cologne, while on tour with La Scala, she starts to record the killing part of Puccini's Turandot. Maria Callas needs to rest, her doctor forbids her to go to Edinburgh with La Scala again for another *Sonnambula*.

With Meneghini outside their home in Milan.

A big quarrel is barely avoided: can she not sing? But if the tickets have all been sold on account of her? And then too, La Scala is La Scala; a tour abroad simply does not allow for trip-ups and accidents en route. The credibility of the theater, of Milan, of Italy is at stake… The manager, Ghiringhelli, will not hear of it and Maria obeys. She goes, sings her four performances and is about to return to Italy when the theater, due to the triumph obtained, adds a fifth performance not provided for in the contract. This time she digs in her heels, refuses to sing and goes to a ball Elsa Maxwell is giving in Venice.

The Scala production of Lucia *on tour in Vienna.*

The heavens split apart. It does not matter that the fifth performance is a triumph for Renata Scotto, the young colleague who stands in for her and who will have a resounding international career: La Scala cries treason and the press has a ball; Elsa Maxwell opens her big mouth and Maria has to face a very unpleasant situation. Furthermore, her fatigue continues.

She has to record *Medea* (a role very close to her heart; a role which is hers alone) after having been obliged to record operas she had never sung in the theater such as *Pagliacci, Bohème,* or *Manon Lescaut*. And she does not in the least feel like going to San Francisco where two roles are scheduled for her which, for a change, are at the opposite poles of her tessitura: the usual *Lucia* and her first Lady Macbeth since La Scala's opening night in 1952 (was it really only five years ago? It seems to have happened in another life). She wires the manager asking if the dates can be put off or if someone else can sub for her in the first performances to give her time to regain her strength. The facts are that she has four performances to sing, that the season is time-bound and consequently the theater cancels her contract, gets a substitute for her and tells her she will never sing again in San Francisco. All hell breaks loose.

Maria is on the brink of a precipice. Does she realize this? Not yet, apparently. Negative signs accumulate, she seems on the verge of a breakdown, but then a concert triumph in Dallas is enough, a happy season-opener in Verdi's *Ballo in Maschera* at La Scala (it is her fifth opening night in seven years) suffices for all the pieces to fall back into place.

His role as Amelia brings her back home to colleagues she loves and who love her – Giulietta Simionato, Ettore Bastianini – and to a conductor like Gianandrea Gavazzeni who has esteemed her for years. The public's dedication moves her and, even if there is a great chill between her and the management because of the Edinburgh incident, the performances in Milan are reviving and give her confidence. Serene, she leaves for Rome where the season opener awaits her – her classic *Norma*.

By now Maria's first nights attract, along with the regular public, celebrities of all kinds and the Rome Opera does not intend to be outdone. Thus for that highly fashionable January 2, 1958 there are movie divas like Anna Magnani, Gina Lollobrigida and Silvana Pampanini, an artistic genius such as

The World and Rome

Arrivals, departures, personalities, hats… In Vienna, Maria is greeted by the great conductor Karl Boehm.

It is not true that I am impulsive and capricious. It is true that I have my exigencies, and how I do. But not for myself, only in order to reach the goal to which I have dedicated my existence: to perpetuate the noble art of grand opera.

Giorgio De Chirico, a goodly helping of politicians and their courtiers and to crown it all, the President of the Republic Giovanni Gronchi. Hence an evening of full press coverage, but Maria has long been accustomed to that. Except that this time she is unwell. Flu is making the rounds in Rome and her Adalgisa, Fedora Barbieri, has fallen victim to it and has to be replaced. Maria feels the warning symptoms waiting in ambush. She had to sing "Casta diva" on television on New Year's Eve and the next day she has no voice. Maria notifies the theater, but just imagine: all the others can be replaced, but that opening is a Callas night, the tickets sold in her name (even to scalpers) and Callas there must be at all costs. Therefore she has to come and sing. The following night, in the name of a professionalism written in her DNA, she comes to the theater well knowing that she just cannot make it. She sings, but not well.

Her "Casta Diva", inimitably and unmistakably her own, is not its usual mother-of-pearl and in the following allegro some notes do not come out at all as they

Imogene and Amelia – two triumphant new roles.

should. In cases of this kind, the public has two possible reactions: either to be affectionate accomplices and loyally gratify the artist in difficulty with some encouraging applause, or else, in the full gladiatorial tradition, turn ferocious, and demand blood.

In Rome the evening is not an auspicious one for Maria Callas. No excessive reactions, but two nasty cat calls from above ("Go back to Milan" and "She is costing us a million") leave no doubts about the mood of the gallery goers and forebode an imminent storm. At that point, Maria decides not to risk it. After all, she was ill, she had warned the theater, she had the right to a stand-in and now it was the time for the stand-in to do her stuff. Let her continue, because Maria was certainly not able to.

And if the stand-in was not there, why had the theater not called her in? All the worse for the theater, for the public, for one and all: her fever, her sore throat, the injections and tranquilizers were bad enough – she had no intention of letting herself be massacred.

It was a very big mistake, because in fact there is no trace of a stand-in at the theater and so, after frenetic negotiations in her dressing room, supplications, shouts and injunctions, the performance has to be suspended and the moral lynching of Maria Callas is about to begin. If nothing else, Maria manages to escape a literal physical lynching by using the underground passage to return directly to the Hotel Quirinale, but for the rest…

If she escapes hearing the whistles and cat calls flying round the auditorium, for the whole night she has a crowd not exactly singing her praises outside the hotel. (The newspaper photos of the time show a depressing sampler of sardonic grins, hands pointing "horns" at her window and ugly faces wearing most ugly expressions). And the morning after they have to tell her that flyers pasted onto the opera house walls read "Callas get out of Rome". Not to mention the newspaper headlines, the discussions in Parliament regarding the "scandal" she has created, and other hysterics.

All of this fuss for a show interrupted after the first act, even if in the presence of the President of the Republic? And yet, it happened. Little does it matter that the President's wife herself phones Maria in reply to a letter of apology. Little does it matter that the facts of the incident showing how correct Maria had been in her behavior and how negligent the theater, become public domain, as do the medical certificates. The theater does not want to hear of Callas,

After the triumph of Il Pirata.

who is eager to do the other performances she has been engaged for, as soon as she is better.

They dismiss her and announced that henceforth Rome is closed to her. At this point she is the one to take legal action, thus complicating the situation even further. (She eventually won the case, of course, but by then years had passed, and her life by then had taken quite a different course.) In the meantime, the story makes the rounds of the press and the general public that perhaps had never even seen or heard her.

Within a few days it is discovered that Maria Callas has stained herself with who knows what crime against – yes, against what exactly? At least against the Italian State, to judge by the uncontrollable wave of reactions – today hardly comprehensible – that this banal incident created in the media. It was the most unpleasant thing that had happened to her up to then – were there really people among the public who hated her that much? – and she suffered from it. The trouble was that she did not realize how much it was going to cost her.

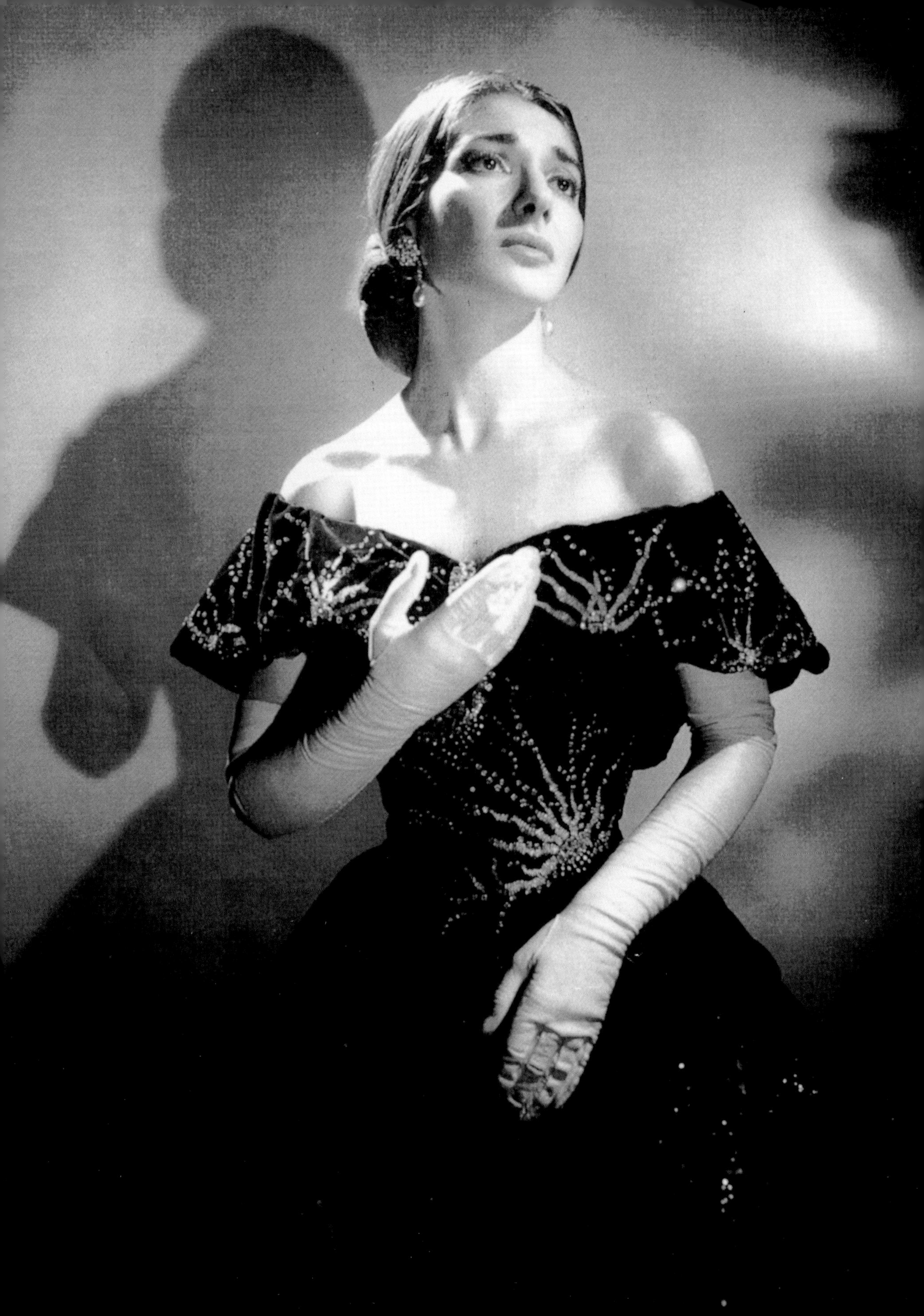

THE NEW LIFE

The "Rome Scandal", as the episode was immediately coined, represented a most serious blow to Maria's public image and definitely marked a dividing line – symbolic if you like – in her career. Among the most unpleasant consequences, certainly, was that half the world's opera houses began to think of her as definitely "problematic" and to withdraw from committing themselves – not without consequences for the most renowned, highest paid, and by now most infamous singer in the world.

The 1957-58 opera season is, in effect, the last true "Callas season", rich in engagements around the world. Twenty days after the Rome row, there is the Chicago concert, followed by the second group of performances at the Met (with the exciting promise of future events from Violetta to Lady Macbeth), a concert in Madrid, a memorable *Traviata* in Lisbon (for many, her best ever) and the desired return to La Scala for *Anna Bolena*, which is the prelude to her last Milanese opening night: Bellini's *Il Pirata*, once again a seldom performed work, once again an admirable cast at her side (Corelli, Bastianini), once again a triumph.

Maria appears thinner than ever before,

I am not obsessed with money nor am I capricious, even if I like beautiful things and do not see why I shouldn't have them after years when I could not even afford to buy a dress.

Prima donnas come and go. La Scala remains!
ANTONIO GHIRINGHELLI

arms bony and hands that seem to mould space, a Renaissance neck and her voice at its best with the right degrees of impetus and sweetness, outbreaks of violence and spells of exhaustion. And yet the La Scala management behaves with hostility, the manager Ghiringhelli – the same who created entire seasons around her name, who had wanted to mount productions with her and for her that had already belonged to the history of the theater – now finds her almost unbearable and, in any case, does not renew her contract.

Does she realize what she is losing? The fact remains that Maria sings her five performances of *Il Pirata* and leaves Milan without knowing if or when she will ever return. The opera ends with another mad scene – one of those which when she sings them seem to combine Gothic romance and Freud, sending even the most blasé of spectators wild with enthusiasm – and at the last performance she makes use of certain words that seem written on purpose for the occasion ("There, do you see, the grim scaffold ") pointing with appropriate gestures to the manager's box, and launching in that direction the final vocal flourishes of a dethroned queen. She arouses such enthusiasm that the crowd, waiting at the stage door, follows her as she goes to dine at Biffi's, throwing a carpet of flowers before her as she walks.

6

> *Madam Callas is constitutionally incapable of inserting herself in any organization that has not been made to measure for her.*
> RUDOLF BING

"Exiled" from Milan (prima donnas and opera fanatics have always used "melodramatic" language), "la Divina" goes to London for concerts and recordings. There she makes two of her most sensational albums: *Verdi Heroines* and *Famous Mad Scenes*, points of reference for singers to come, worldwide bestsellers still today; but in the former, the purely vocal results are uneven and in Abigaille's cabaletta Maria bestows on posterity a top note which is a distinct scream.

She chalks up a *Traviata* at Covent Garden whose phrasing is perhaps the most ingenious ever, makes an American concert tour and in Dallas alternates *Traviata* (it will be her last, but who can imagine it – Maria least of anyone) with *Medea*. But she cannot come to terms with Bing, the agreement for her future New York dates does not work out (and this time it is a series of twenty-six performances, no less, including a new *Macbeth* which she is very keen on) and the exasperated manager gives up the whole affair. Callas, once again, is in the eye of the hurricane: capricious, hateful and undependable…

In reality all she asked was to move two *Traviata* dates so that they did not fall too close to *Macbeth* – had she too begun to note that her voice could no longer take on everything with impunity? – but that is the fact: "La Callas" is a prisoner of a public image which is absolutely out of her control. To miss out on the Met is a heartache, but the consolation is very near: little more than a month later, December 19, 1958, Maria encounters one of the great, true loves of her life: Paris.

Maria with the wife of Onassis.

Her debut at the Opéra – a gala evening in the presence of the President of the Republic (once again…) René Coty and an audience of the kind only Paris at that time could draw – is really a curious pot-pourri: Selections from *Norma*, *Trovatore* and the *Barber* in the first half. Then an intermission with prizes (among them a super-luxurious SIMCA automobile "as homage to the Prima Donna") followed by the second act of *Tosca*.

Maria takes it all seriously, sings well even if at times a bit dryly, creates line, style, phrasing and intensity which at the Opéra then must seem perhaps to come from another planet. (The French style of singing at that time, we should never forget, was at Europe's lowest levels and quite unworthy of the great theater capital that Paris certainly was.) With one blow she conquers a city, a public, a "circle".

The occasion – on which even the maids of

The New Life

honor are dressed by Dior and Givenchy, Balmain, Cardin or Nina Ricci – has gathered together the biggest names of international society which begins to exert an ever greater fascination on Maria and was soon to become her natural habitat. Among aristocrats and magnates there were writers like Cocteau and Sagan, artists like Chaplin, Gérard Philippe and Michèle Morgan, as well as some Greeks who came in homage to their compatriot. One of them was Aristotle Onassis, one of the world's richest men. However all that may be, that gala represented the close of 1958 for Maria. The next year found her engaged in various concerts and recordings, but on only eleven occasions did she sing a complete opera. Two concert performances of *Il Pirata* in New York and Washington; five of *Medea* in London and, in Dallas, two each of *Lucia* (the last…) and *Medea* again.

What was happening? To begin with, her vocal exhaustion had broken all at once; and though in past months perhaps a few weeks of rest were enough to set things right, by now the signs of an incipient decline seemed inevitable. From then on, Maria would experience varying voice and power from one occasion to the next, the state of her nerves affecting her breath control and emission more or less noticeably, but by then the top notes wavered and cracked and a scream was lurking in ambush so that, depending upon the situation, she would decide at the last moment whether or not to close certain pieces (e.g. the aria from *La Vestale*) with a top note, or a more prudent lower note.

Unfortunately it is precisely during this period that certain of her performances begin to be broadcast on television and today constitute her far too limited patrimony in images. No one would ever see her at the peak of her vocal glory when her instrument was considered incomparable, no one would be able to study the genius of her acting constructed around her body, her gestures, her face.

What would remain was the dubious testimony of her Paris debut wearing a costume that could not become anyone, and a visible absence of stage direction; and then, a few concerts where she creates her own staging with an admirable play of hands and eyes. Too little, of course, and with the remains of a voice which, if still capable of

With "Ari".

It is better to sing for ten years so intensely and incomparably as Maria Callas did, than to sing for almost thirty years as I have done.
Beverly Sills

I got myself a bad reputation only because I defended music and my professional integrity.

moments of true glory, already gave cause to regret the true Callas voice.

If one adds the series of "scandals," the reputation of "troublemaker" (which, after all, was only the proud defense of her professionalism), the very high level of her fees (but the theaters' box-office takings were in proportion), and we have the world's most celebrated singer incredibly short on engagements, with far too many doors closed to her. In 1959 Maria Callas does not even sing thirty performances. In 1960 there are only seven – just seven, but at least there is different reason for this.

The reason is Onassis. Some months after the Paris engagement, Onassis had gone to London, in June 1959, to hear her in *Medea*, taking with him a veritable court of millionaire friends. Onassis who throws her a party straight out of the *Arabian Nights*, Onassis who invites her on a cruise for the following month. Maria, with no professional dates, hesitates and then accepts, succumbing to the kindly solicitations of the shipping magnate's wife as well. Thus, on July 22, 1959, she and Titta embark on the "Christina", a million-dollar yacht, where they are met by the other cruise "attraction", Winston and Lady Churchill.

If the "Rome Scandal" had made Maria Callas's name known far beyond musical and cultural circles generally, even in places where the news of the "rivalry with Tebaldi" had not reached, "the cruise on the Christina" had an effect on the collective imagination of the late fifties and early sixties which probably today is hardly comprehensible.

The facts could not be simpler. Maria, thirty-six years of age (Only just? Yes, only just. Like all great predestined women, whether Marilyn Monroe, Judy Garland, Edith Piaf or Billie Holiday, she seems to have already consumed several lifetimes), married for a decade to a much older father-impresario husband, she falls in love with another man. Nothing more or less than that. But like her, he is also married. He is

Callas's legendary eyes.

Triggered from the depths a searing voice, deep, high, strident, supernatural, baroque, a voice like no other had attempted, to fight death. A miraculous voice, that of a genius...
YVES SAINT-LAURENT

The New Life

something like the wealthiest man in the world, and she, a tabloid celebrity.

He overwhelms the imagination of an Italy on the threshold of the Great Boom, with images of absolutely unthinkable luxury (possibly a little vulgar), while she is suspected of witchcraft because of her rages and sensational diet, barbaric sentiments (poor Maria, come to think of it...) and brilliant conquests, ostentatious opulence (how many well-off Milanese, seeing her in the magazines with her sets of pearls, rubies or emeralds, which in succession mark each of her La Scala triumphs, remember her in those shapeless overcoats, horrid little hats with veils to hide her swollen face, greasy hair and pimply skin! And that was just yesterday, just six or seven years ago.)

On the seas of Greece, the summer of 1959 brings Maria the second great love of her life. If Titta was a refuge and salvation for a big girl with an oversized ego and some equally devastating complexes, this time the relationship is – at least in theory – on an equal plane. And, according to witnesses,

I owe everything to my husband and for him I would give my career and my life. (1957)

With Grace Kelly; jet-setting is Maria's new world.

sexual attraction plays the preponderant role. In this field he already has a solid reputation. She, it appears, is at the end of eight years of abstention out of ten years of marriage. Whether true or not matters little, but backstage gossip is for years the prime source of news about the "cruise on the Christina". The essential thing is that a flame has been lit, and for Maria it is definitive.

Because this "impossible" woman has, among other qualities, basic honesty, a moral integrity that today is admired but which at the time only added fuel to the scandal. (What a love of scandal it was in Italy in those days! Just look at the newspaper headlines – and not only in the popular press. It was the "Onassis Scandal" primarily in provincial

With Tito Gobbi, another beautiful scene.

Last flickers at La Scala: Medea once again.

post-war Italy, whereas abroad, the sensation was due more to the coupling of two famous names, with the dropping of the Meneghini in the diva's last name hardly worrying anyone.)

We only have to look at the dates: Maria and Titta get to the Onassises on July 22, 1959 and, before mid-August Maria lets her husband know that she is in love with someone else. On September 8 the Meneghinis jointly announce they are separating by common consent. No subterfuges and no compromises. In November, in Brescia, the separation is made legal and the newsreels show Callas flying to Italy between Dallas performances of *Lucia* and *Medea*, literally besieged by crowds, very tense and troubled. But once the legal complications are settled, aside from the press campaign unleashed against her in Italy, and from the persecution of photographers who tail her everywhere, for Maria it is truly the beginning of a new life.

Opera lovers, the most unconditioned

I have been singing for twenty-three years, but for some time it has become a torture. They wait in ambush for me, they will not forgive me a cold, a raw note. Sing? Yes, but for myself, for my pleasure. The public is a monster. (1960)

fanatics, do not seem to realize completely that in those months Maria Callas virtually ceases to exist as a singer. Certainly for a long time the world press has been full of reports on her cancelled engagements, disputes with this or that theater, of her being dethroned at La Scala and invective in New York. Though had there not always been news, on the other hand, of triumphs in this or that American or European city? Were there not photos everywhere of her, with her hair sleeked into an elegant chignon; Maria bedecked in furs and jewels, showered with flowers; glimpses of those legendary flashing eyes? Were her recordings not released regularly?

And the drum beats about new operatic projects, new prestigious productions resounding through almost all the world's newspapers – not on the arts pages, mind you, but in the news sections where columns on Liz Taylor or Ava Gardner appeared. And yet in the early sixties, the Callas voice is absent, is a ghost except for the recording sessions (but Maria vetoes the release of almost all the recordings in that period), and a few television appearances.

For the rest, there are seven public appearances in 1960, as mentioned; six in 1961, eight in 1962, six in 1963. The remaining

I have no more desire to sing. I want to live, live like any other woman. (1962)

The New Life

time Maria spends traveling around the world, on cruises, at Montecarlo, in Paris or Greece, on the French Riviera. She is rarely in her Milan apartment, and she is soon to leave it definitively for Paris, Avenue Foch, the street of the jetsetters. After a few years she would move to her final home in the equally prestigious Avenue Georges Mandel.

In those four years there is only one artistic event worthy of her: the reconciliation with La Scala, which results in one more season opening at Sant'Ambrogio and, again, it makes history. On December 7, 1960 the première of Donizetti's *Poliuto* returns Maria to her public and is her last stage debut in an opera new to her. There is not the expected Luchino as stage director, but there are trusted colleagues like Corelli and Bastianini. Her new friends are scattered throughout the auditorium (besides Onassis, the Beghun and Grace Kelly) and the gallery, her gallery, applauds movingly as she enters the stage. Those sitting up there have not heard her for more than two years.

They see she is excessively thin, truly emaciated, and extremely tense, nervous. The voice? A ghost of itself, very much smaller and sometimes uncertain (Uncertain? Callas?!). With sublime moments, of course, with a fragility, a pathos that endears, but with such signs of fatigue and – how can one deny it? – at least one top note that is one of the most impossible notes imaginable. But it does not matter. Maria was there, Maria is singing at La Scala again, and it is a triumph.

She returns the next year for one more *Medea*, which will be her final La Scala appearance. In the meantime, in that handful of performances that make up her activity

By now photos of Maria are taken almost exclusively at balls and social events.

> *The singing of Medea-Callas is speech-singing, sometimes shouted, at other times suffocated or ending in a croak, but always tensely nervous: in substance, expressionistic. At times priestly, at times ferocious as a beast that paws the ground in devouring the last bits of its meal. With this Medea, Maria Callas creates a great Art Nouveau figure.*
> EUGENIO MONTALE

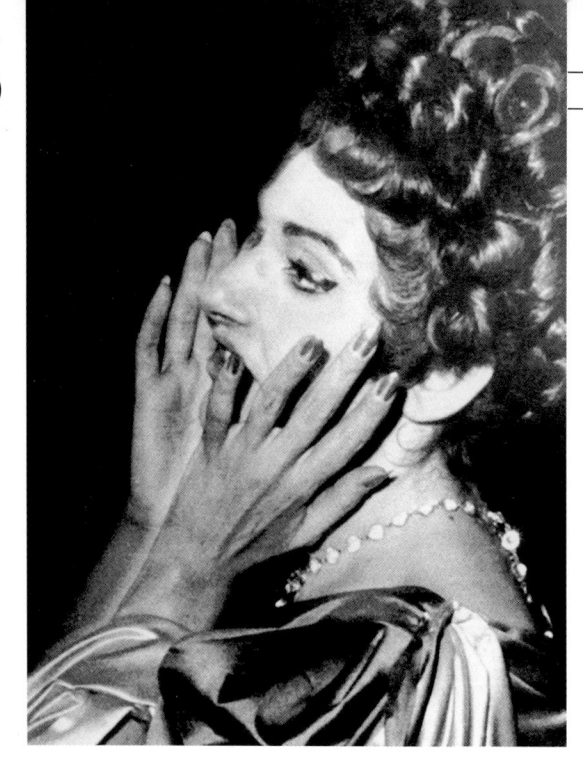

As Paolina in Poliuto, *her last opening at La Scala.*

from 1960-63, there are some concerts in which for the first time she sings pieces of an ambiguous tessitura bordering on mezzo soprano (the arias of Cenerentola and Eboli, Massenet's Chimène and Carmen) in the attempt to limit the damages to her top register; two performances at the amphitheater at Epidaurus, *Norma* one year, *Medea* the next.

And those old La Scala fans who can afford to, spurred by Italian writer Alberto Arbasino, take advantage of those first charter flights and rush to hear her. And among the recordings that remain unreleased, two highly prestigious ones dedicated to the French repertoire where she once more alternates between contralto and light soprano pieces running into sharp high notes that are decidedly horrifying at times (the "Jewel Song" from *Faust!*) but at the same time, weaving that magic of phrasing that never ceases to astonish and seduce.

Nevertheless, though her voice has been silent far too long, and lack of practice has aggravated the natural process of aging, at a certain point Maria makes up her mind to start again from scratch. She studies, vocalizes, comes to terms with a compromised and reduced voice, regains some steadiness, flexibility and evens out her registers. She feels ready to make a comeback in a big way, and so she does.

London, Covent Garden, a stage director who is mad about her (Zeffirelli), a colleague with whom she gets on beautifully (Tito Gobbi): she is Tosca, and subsequently, after a few months, even Norma in Paris, her city of residence. She makes the two albums which bring her back to artistic prominence (as for social prominence, in which she apparently untiringly lavishes, there can never be enough). It is a strong sign of revival: this time she really means it. As for the rest, we will see.

With Franco Corelli in Poliuto.

> *Movements, eyes, gestures, hands… Her smile makes you go off your head: it is just like that of certain ironic classical statues.*
> ALBERTO ARBASINO

BEFORE SILENCE

When Maria Callas returns to sing in *Tosca* at Covent Garden, it is obvious to everyone that a change has come over the way the public relates to her. Her long silence (it has been two years since her last "première," *Medea* at La Scala in December 1961); the crazed prominence the media has given to her private life; the rumors, ever more alarming, of the condition of her voice (not to mention her nerves), trigger expectations and uncertainties of all kinds – and all of them excessive – forming a mixture which, to say the least, is explosive.

She is vaguely aware of all this and throws herself into the undertaking with all her energy – which, moreover, is neither a great deal, nor intact. Her voice, for example, has distinctly improved and we can say it is generally under control. But a single note going astray at any point in the score could be enough to prove that this, by now, is a *different* voice, not the voice that has made Maria into "la Callas".

In addition, the psycho-physical condition of "la Divina" is, without exaggerating, precarious, with sudden spells of weakness alternating with high blood pressure and a stubborn determination to vindicate herself,

Tosca, the role of her last apparitions.

giving way to fits of panic. And yet, with the help of an even more magnetic stage presence and a look that exalts her (of which photos and posters immediately circulate throughout the world), along with an insistent and widespread publicity campaign, it is precisely the physical and vocal image of the 1964-65 Callas that becomes an enduring icon long into the future.

In a word, on January 21, 1964, Maria wins her wager: on points after the first act, easily after the second, and triumphantly by the end of the opera. The excitement unleashed with her entrance onto the stage seems

---

The socialite of the slick magazines has nothing in common with the person we knew on the job, but whom many imagine to be like the former.
GIANANDREA GAVAZZENI

With Franco Corelli again, her frequent partner during her final performances.

overwhelming, even to those who have followed her for years. The electricity that is felt in the hall seems almost to transmit itself to the public, and to such an extent that the enthusiastic reaction turns into a kind of immense hysteria.

The seven performances of *Tosca* at Covent Garden give her wings. The audience seems to have gone crazy, she becomes her old self again, regains confidence, and by the fifth performance begins to have fun. She gives everything she has got. Zeffirelli has regulated her subtly expressive gestures and put her into costumes that make her beautiful. In the second act, Tito Gobbi stimulates her with a performance that often turns on spur-of-the-moment inspiration and this incites her into giving as good as she gets. She even exploits her myopia to increase the pathos of certain moments.

This Tosca of hers is described, commented upon, analyzed gesture by gesture, scene by scene: the range of looks and blandishments she can produce in the first act; how she tries to escape from Scarpia's rape attempts in the second, running, tripping, literally groping her way to the room in Palazzo Farnese recreated in claustrophobic splendor by Renzo Mongiardino's sets (the description of certain moments still recurs, for example, in Arbasino's memoirs thirty-five years later); the savagery with which she stabs Scarpia, the goose flesh her declamation produces at act end, the throes of her despair before her suicide…

> *Her way of acting was always opposite to the conventional way, an intense and electric dialog with the public. It was truth, love, suffering, life.*
> CAMILLA CEDERNA

At the last performance the second act is broadcast on television and certain newspapers go so far as to print some photographic sequences that reconstruct the scene. In short, a great victory, and so what if in all the critiques the most controversial aspects, the strictly vocal ones, are everywhere brought up and handled more or less gallantly, more or less remorselessly. London now conquered, Maria prepares to lay siege to Paris. But first she records an impressive number of arias for EMI, some of which are released the following year, others in 1972, and still others, never.

Then she performs in *Norma* at the Opéra so that after the curious 1958 gala and a subsequent recital, the Parisian public too can finally say it has heard Maria Callas, or what is left of her, in a full opera. She harks back to one of her cult roles. Can she still defend it? Yes, in part, in certain phrases, in certain lacerating inflections. Is it a reduced version? From a strictly vocal point of view, yes, of course. However much she has managed to put her vocal apparatus right, the voice is still irreversibly compromised. Still, all in all, the old magic works and the performances are a success to the point that a return is planned for the following year.

Now the essential thing is to keep on trying, and indeed Maria's life is nothing but a series of projects for Paris, Milan, New York and London: *Traviata* (does she seriously think she can still sing it?), *Anna Bolena*, *Macbeth*, *Tosca*, again and even *L'incoronazione di Poppea*, all to be done with the biggest names on the market, of course: Karajan, Luchino still and always, Zeffirelli, the young Prêtre who has had his eye on her in the last years, the very young Teresa Berganza, whom she likes so much.

Meanwhile she records *Carmen* in a curious version where she alternates between soprano and mezzo soprano according to the piece (and at times even within a piece), light colors and very dark inflections that in the end compose a most curious patchwork with which there is not much comparison. And, in fact, the reactions to it are diametrically opposed: some find it sublime, others execrable. Thus, the last seven months of 1964 are divided between a project and a cruise, constant study, and a new recording of *Tosca*. Indeed there is a movie in the works directed by Zeffirelli and a sound track is needed that meets up-to-date stereo requirements. In the end, for a complicated problem of rights, nothing is ever made.

A Tosca like that had never been seen. It spoiled my pleasure in that opera, because I never again managed to appreciate any other artist after hearing her.
RUDOLF BING

Norma, the last time.

After Luchino, Pierpaolo, her new mentor/demiurge.

And so we reach 1965, the final year of Maria's career even if no one including Maria herself could imagine it. The Paris *Tosca* is a success, we can even call it a triumph, despite the fact that many ask themselves where the voice has gone to. It does not sound like Callas. Is it possible? Yes, it is. In her constantly growing anxiety to keep control of it, Maria seems almost to hold it back. Certainly the risk of ugly notes is diminished, but… What remains is the icon, and from some standpoints that is sufficient.

One need only listen to any pirated recording to hear what happens as soon as she steps onto the stage in the two performances of *Tosca* which she goes to sing in New York seven years after her last appearance at the Metropolitan: "Mario, Mario, Mario!" she declaims imperiously from off stage; "Son qui," responds Franco Corelli/Cavaradossi who goes to the church door to let her in and, at the mere appearance of Maria/Tosca, the entire house explodes into a limitless roar, three thousand voices in unison hurl at her an avalanche of bestial howls, love, fanaticism.

Reactions of this kind would be enough to allay any doubts about the magical power Callas wielded over her public. And it was with this spirit, this force inside of her that she went to confront the revival of *Norma* in May at the Paris Opéra. This time, however, everything goes against her: malaise, a temporary loss of voice, a few treacherous notes that crack on certain evenings, and the unbearable sensation that her voice is not responding, that it is going its own way, changing texture, color, everything, from one scene to the next, from one minute to the next.

In five performances everything possible

I enjoy battling with the crowd, but on the condition that I am in full possession of my powers.

Cheerful and relaxed on the set of Medea.

happens and photos go round the world of Callas worn out, Callas in a half-faint, Callas so exhausted that she cannot keep her eyes open before the camera; and the drums beat out news that changes from one evening to the next: Callas booed, Callas triumphs, Callas faints, Callas makes it to the end thanks only to injections given her between the acts, Callas never before in such great form, Callas reunited with Simionato (the beloved Giulietta is her Adalgisa for only two performances), Callas stops the performance after the third act… Under these circumstances, it is unthinkable to do the four scheduled performances of *Tosca* at Covent Garden; she sings only one, and is obliged to choose the one on July 5 because the royal family is to be present and it is best not to offend the Crown.

After which, nothing. One last *Tosca*, and for eight years the world's most legendary voice is silent. Not that Callas lacks for offers, quite the contrary. Even though knowing that her voice has lost much of its power, even while aware that she has become more

> *I have always asked myself how it was possible that a personality whose drug was life on the stage could have survived psychologically and physically the definitive rupture in 1965 with what was her true mission.*
> WERNER SCHROETER

difficult, more exigent perhaps than ever, theater managers still put their hopes in her witch-like ability to ignite the public, to create an event. The offers follow one after the other, the press refers to contracts in the offing with London or New York, maybe Paris, or… But nothing more would ever come of it.

There are even some, like Visconti, who suggest new directions, new horizons envisioning her in a world of Strauss (*Salome*,

With Olympics champion Giuseppe Gentile making his movie debut.

the Marschallin in *Rosenkavalier*), tempting her with languages she has never ventured into before (maybe Janacek?). And some, much more sensibly, urge her to take that most singular Carmen of hers onto the stage which, thus far, she has only sung on records – that Carmen whose dark side, she, Maria, could portray like no one else: the death impulse, the anxiety for freedom, the somber sense of mystery, of atavistic predestination, of inexorable fate. But she wants none of it. She cannot see herself with castanets dancing on tabletops say the press gossips.

In reality, the proud Maria, the perfectionist Maria, the Maria without pity for herself, feels that if she is to continue singing, she must do so in her repertory of old which brought her glory. Would Carmen be a role within her reach today? She wants to sing Violetta again.

I might be capable of killing if my freedom were taken away.

Would certain roles, ambiguous in tessitura, bordering on the mezzo, be distinctly convenient for her?

She knows, she feels it herself, to be a soprano and she will not accept compromises. It would be like admitting that the world's greatest, the only real living legend of the world of opera, is no longer up to the mark. So then, yes, let's speak about work, let's consider new productions, but only in our usual roles: Norma, Violetta, Tosca, Lady Macbeth… Also because, meanwhile, right there before her eyes, at least two voices have exploded onto the scene that could truly put her into the shade on the international scene.

Already for several years, first in London and New York, but then immediately afterwards and powerfully in Italy and the rest of the world, Joan Sutherland has been imposing the marvels of her stellar and absolutely incomparable virtuosity. She who had sung the part of Clotilde, Norma's confidante, at Maria's side in a 1952 London production – thus a bit part, not even a second lead – today is singing Lucia all over

> *It was Maria who inspired me when I was starting my career and she never stopped encouraging me and pushing me to do the things Richard Bonynge and I have tried to do.*
> — JOAN SUTHERLAND

the world, working up fanatical enthusiasm and, above all, singing it in a way that is by now forever closed to Maria, with a technical mastery, a fantastic facility of ornamentation, that is not only making a legend of her but is actually making history.

And then too, Sutherland has just added *Norma* to her repertory, Sutherland has the doors of La Scala open to her, Sutherland is steadily recording, not only all of Maria's roles (Lucia, Violetta, Amina, Elvira and even Norma), but Mozart and Handel as well. She gives spectacular recitals brimming with rarities that range from the Baroque to Verdi without neglecting French opera and operetta, Neo-classicism, Romanticism and salon pieces! A *diva assoluta* and moneymaker in all parts of the globe, Sutherland is obviously mad about Maria. She has studied and studied her again, has received her applause and good wishes at that London performance of *Lucia* which has ultimately revealed her to the world.

She wants to follow in Maria's footsteps, though perhaps is not even aware herself that in some ways she has already surpassed Maria, at least on the question of technique and virtuosity, breadth of repertory and demand from theaters… Certainly Sutherland does not and never will have Maria's interpretative genius, the miraculous elasticity of phrase, the soul, the pathos, the hypnotic power, the acting ability, but… but opera is made with the voice, and the vocal standards of the Australian giantess are off-limits to Maria by now.

Just as they are, furthermore, with regard to the new star, only just born but destined to conquer the world with lightning speed: Montserrat Caballé, a Spanish soprano not even terribly young who has spent years in the ranks (like Sutherland, for that matter, both of them have burst upon the scene at thirty-two, thirty-three years of age) who imposes something like a magical spell on the opera aficionados of half the world with a

> *Without wanting to imitate the inimitable, I always, following Maria Callas's example, try to make come to life the masterpieces of a past which she taught us to understand.*
> — MONTSERRAT CABALLÉ

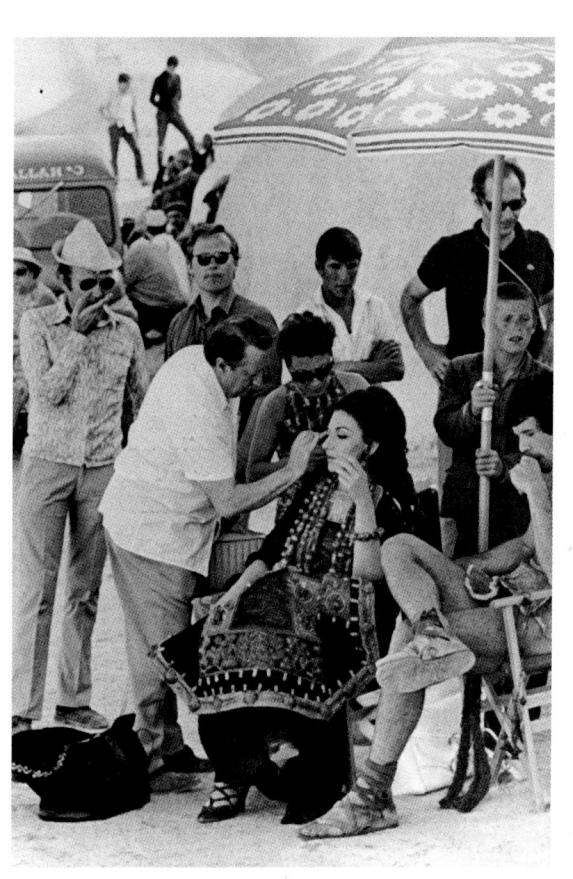

In the torrid Turkish heat wearing the heavy costume of the Colchis witch.

That look, as searching as ever.

voice of incomparable beauty, impalpable, even celestial.

And if there is even talk of a Callas/Sutherland combination (*Les Hugenots* at La Scala, in which Maria could have the part of Valentina, in the end prudently given to Giulietta Simionato, while Sutherland might take care of the fantastical coloratura of Queen Margherita di Valois, as precisely what occurs), Caballé ends up singing all those roles which opera buffs want to hear Maria do: *Lucrezia Borgia*, of course, with its alternation of ecstatic sweetness and bouts of violent invective; *Maria Stuarda*, with that last act in which the protagonist loops one pre-finale into another, in a tour de force consented to only a very few; the Elisabetta of *Roberto Devereux*, ferocious and apocalyptic in its choleric rages with a finale as grandiose as that of *Anna Bolena*.

Meanwhile, as her colleagues monopolize the world's most important theaters (with Leontyne Price quite incomparable and firmly installed in the late Verdi roles for her vocal splendor and insolence of projection – which is to say, another path barred to Callas) Maria drifts into the rhythms of the nomadic international jet set. Cruises, balls, charity galas moving from Paris to Montecarlo, the Mediterranean, and who knows where else. She is once again in all the newspapers when on September 17, 1968 she attends the season opening of the Metropolitan in New York: *Adriana Lecouvreur* sung by Renata Tebaldi. At the end of the performance Rudolf Bing accompanies her to her old rival's dressing room: embraces, handholding, photos cheek-to-cheek, palpable emotion on both parts.

The rivalry between us was created by the press. Today I can say that it brought us both a lot of publicity and that it was good for opera.
RENATA TEBALDI

Neither is Renata her old self, certainly, but she is still singing and her public adores her.

And Maria? Is she still studying? It seems so. Has she given up all intentions of a career? Officially, certainly not. But within herself, who knows? Perhaps if her private situation were stabilized legally… but time passes, Onassis cannot make up his mind and suddenly, without notice, he stabs her in the back: on October 22, 1968 the world's richest man marries one of the female symbols of the times: Jacqueline Bouvier, the widow Kennedy.

Little does it matter that rather than a marriage it is a contract with clauses and counter clauses: Maria is wounded all the same on a personal level, humiliated in the eyes of the world. On the evening of the wedding (which naturally mobilized the world press and would do so for years) she appears in public, beautiful and dressed in *gran soirée* Chez Maxim's in Paris. A bitchy but chic remark is attributed to her ("Mrs. Kennedy has done well to give her children a grandfather"), but those close to her say she was devastated, drained of all energy, listless.

On the professional level, at least, the shock gives her the push needed to get going.

She throws herself headlong into study, goes again for lessons to eighty-year-old Elvira de Hildago, the great teacher of her debuts, and the press talks of engagements in Dallas, San Francisco, Paris. Within a few months she returns to the recording studio to make an album of Verdi arias for EMI (*I Lombardi alla Prima Crociata*, *The Sicilian Vespers*, *Attila*, *Il Corsaro*; but she dislikes them and once again refuses to authorize their release, although the results are clearly better than the recordings of 1961 or 1962).

She drafts the terms of her first movie contract. Having missed opportunities with Visconti and Zeffirelli which were the subject of so much talk; having refused Joseph Losey's offer (the role with her in mind in *Boom* went to Elizabeth Taylor), this time she makes up her mind. The role – Medea – is hers like no other, the director might be awkward and rather "suspect" but he enjoys great intellectual prestige. This is Pier Paolo Pasolini, and if nothing else, Maria owes a

After years of tense relations, her moving encounter with her old rival Renata Tebaldi.

legend. He stimulates her, offers her new views on a character that Maria long ago made her own, almost ferociously so. For the film *Medea* he asks her to work on two levels: on the one hand the barbarous sorceress, and on the other the "civilized" Greek woman who has to place herself into Jason's world. She is electrified by it: finally, once again, someone who speaks her language. The work proceeds serenely: the "terrible" Callas wins over everyone with merriment and simplicity, the desire to learn and (as always) extreme professionalism.

Without too much commotion she finds her place among the Pasolini clan (she makes a trip to Africa with him and Alberto Moravia); she is surrounded by newspaper men and is photographed while making up, and on the set, as she eats a sandwich seated wherever she happens to be, while exchanging affectionate kisses on the lips with Pier Paolo. In the director's entourage there are some

---

In the meantime, Maria sang, and the more sublime she was, the more she seemed to be asking for mercy.
PIER PAOLO PASOLINI

---

lovely period of rebirth to him.

The shooting takes up June and July of 1969, first near Ankara, then Aleppo, Grado, Pisa, Anzio and Rome. Pasolini puts her with an actor who is a fetish of the Italian cinema, Massimo Girotti (also among Visconti's favorites) and in the role of Jason, the Olympic champion Giuseppe Gentile, he too making his film debut. Above all he gives her his intellectual temper, his poetic sensibility, and a human gentleness that quickly turns to affection.

He knows nothing of her work as a singer, has never seen her on the stage, but is touched by her voice, by her woman's sensibility and, in short, intrigued by her

who claim she is in love with him, as she had been with Visconti, another homosexual of genius, another demiurge who helped her to change skin. In any case, the essential thing is that Maria is well and happy, totally committed, and that the work exalts her.

Would she sing in the movie? No, absolutely not. Or perhaps she would sing a grave song composed especially for the film, a short chant, archaic and mysterious… This is enough to cause shivers in the opera buffs all over the world. But when the film is released, Maria's voice is heard only in the infrequent dialogs, and then only in the English and French versions. In Italian she is dubbed by Rita Savagnone.

> *Pasolini and I talk a lot.
> He has a very ingenuous way
> of expressing himself, which,
> in the end, is very poetic.*

However that may be, the film brings out a strong and charismatic presence, and Pasolini offers her magnificently intense close-ups, glorifying her eyes to the hilt, the play of her glances, a kind of totemic stare. But the total result is not something that can appeal to the tastes of the average moviegoer, it is not commercially viable. Callas or no Callas, *Medea* is a flop. For Maria it is a disappointment and her film career ends with this first attempt. More discouragement, more closing herself up.

The year 1970 goes by with almost nothing to tell: a trip to Moscow to sit on the jury of the Tschaikowsky Competition; a few sorties into society; a memorable appearance at La Scala with Wally Toscanini for the season opening of *I Vespri Siciliani* with the lead being sung by Renata Scotto whose performance is contested. And then an annoying appearance in the scandal pages, just what she did not need: presumed suicide attempts, immediately denied, and documented visits of Onassis to her Paris apartment. Indeed, despite his matrimonial contract with the widow Kennedy, he seems unwilling to interrupt his friendship with Maria – at least not before she (they say) throws him howling out of the house.

On the professional front, 1971 finds her undertaking what is the typical activity of so many retired opera singers: a series of master classes. She, of course, does not see it in that light and, when the subject of her future

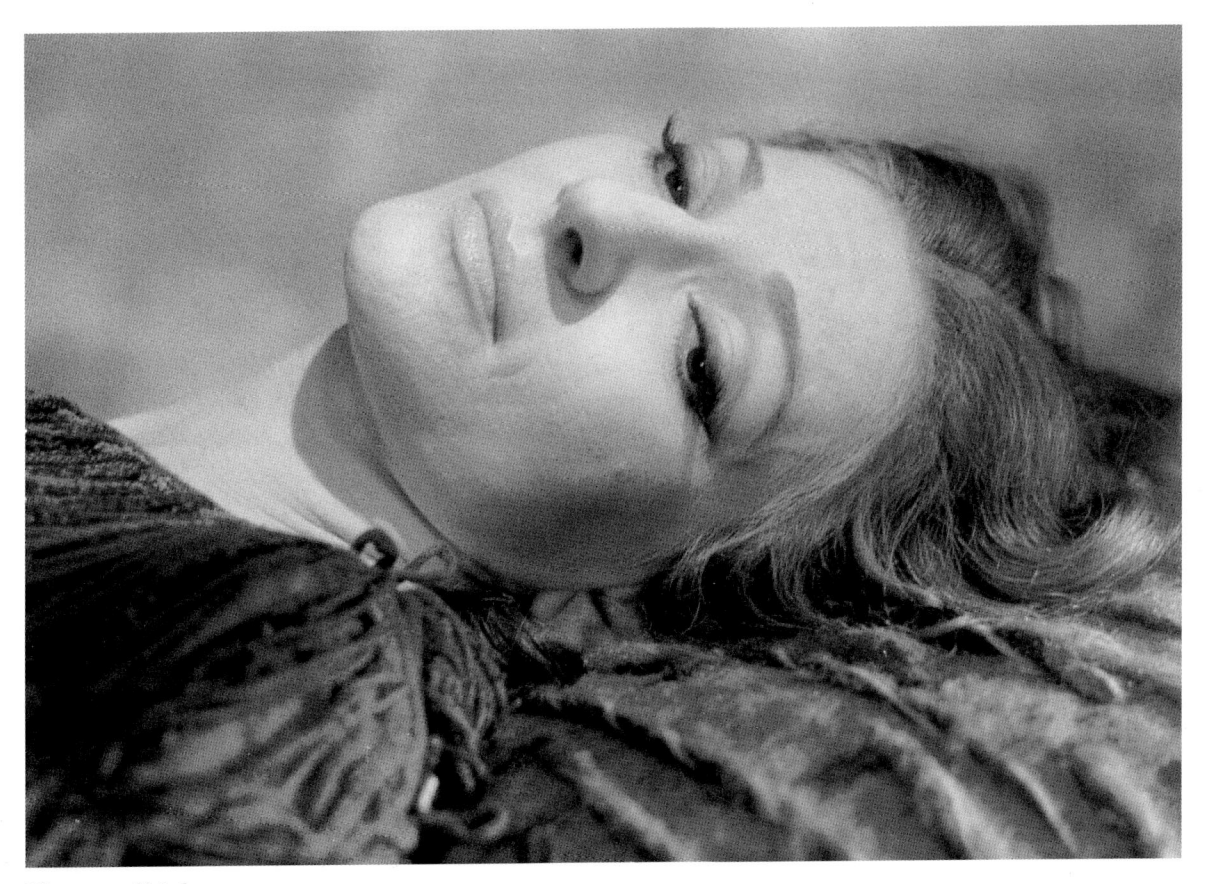

The rages of Medea.

One must vibrate! Vibrate like a violin!

projects in the theater comes up, she insists that she is just waiting for the right occasion. In any case, her first attempt of this kind is a fiasco. It is not Maria's fault. The students chosen to participate in February in Philadelphia are not up to the mark and the courses are interrupted at once.

Things go better at the Juilliard School in New York in October and November, and then in February and March of 1972. With twenty-six young singers selected from three hundred and fifty applicants, Maria indulges herself in the pleasure of speaking about music, delving deep into character analyses, handing down her personal experiences, telling anecdotes and, unexpectedly, singing. In public. And then, because a crowd of auditors are regularly present at the lessons, among them some great singers, musicians, journalists, and others of the profession. For them, for her students and certainly for herself, Maria sings, hums, does snatches of arias, phrases, passages, ranging from the soprano to the bass registers.

Many of these classes are recorded and many years after her death were released commercially by EMI in CD. Here, in addition to the roles Norma and Lucia, she can be heard singing the parts of Scarpia and Philipp II! Transcribed, her discourses were later published. But most importantly in 1994 they inspired one of playwright Terrence McNally's best pieces: *Master Class*, translated and produced worldwide, interpreted by the most prestigious actresses from Zoe Caldwell to Patti LuPone, Faye Dunaway, Rossella Falk and Fanny Ardant, all of whom wanted to become the legendary Maria incarnate, at least for two hours each evening.

She, in the meantime, seems to have found at last "the occasion" she had tried so hard to find, in order to begin seriously singing again. This time, however, it is not a *Traviata* with Visconti in Paris, nor even the project with Karajan in Vienna, nor the *Tosca* movie with Zeffirelli or the debut in Menotti's *The Consul* (a role which she would have performed marvelously). No, the occasion presents itself in the guise of Giuseppe Di Stefano, her companion of so many adventures, who looks her up in New York between Juilliard courses, meets with her, and literally overwhelms her.

The legendary team of the fifties, he says, can – more so, *must* – get together again. Of course, the voices are not quite what they once were, and Di Stefano's has in fact gone more to ruin than Maria's. But both of them need an audience, both of them need to show the world that they are still on top, and both of them have ghosts to exorcise: for Maria it is the loss of Onassis and her loneliness; for Di Stefano it is a tumor that is carrying his twenty-year-old daughter away from him. Both in fragile condition, but with outsized egos, they join forces and a desperation to fulfill what would be Maria's last adventure – and certainly the saddest.

A face serving as an icon for the 20th Century.

THE RETURN

Finding Di Stefano again is, for Maria, a true lifesaver. Under his prodding she decides to get going again. And by comparison with the preceding years it seems that her artistic career can really begin again. To try out her voice, to regain confidence in her strength (and, above all, to master her weaknesses) she makes dates for a series of recordings in anticipation of an album of duets with her one-time partner.

In London at the end of November 1972 for some twenty days she is flanked by the Philips recording technicians, the director De Almeida, and Di Stefano, in the effort to collect enough material – and enough good material. Not an easy task. For differing reasons the two legendary stars have been ground down by unrelenting, intense careers (she), and too little basic technique (he).

Maria's results are also compromised by too long a silence, weakened muscles and diaphragm, while Di Stefano's are undone by irreparable damage that can only be partially compensated for with overall emphatics which, for some, creates the illusion of vigor. Under these circumstances, if the duets from *Otello*, *Don Carlos* and *La Forza del Destino* are concluded to everyone's satisfaction, that is not the case with *Aida* and so the material on hand is too meager to fill both sides of an LP.

But ultimately what is important is to have begun again. Now Maria, who during the recording sessions receives news of her father's death, has a new job facing her: her first staging at the opening of Turin's newly reconstructed Teatro Regio thirty-seven years after it was destroyed by fire. The chosen work is Verdi's *I Vespri Siciliani*. Maria knows it, of course, having sung it in Florence and at La Scala, but… can it be considered a suitable piece for a directing debut? Certainly not.

A choral opera, a vast historical fresco among Verdi's most complex, it needs among other things, a steady and expert hand to manage the movement of large groups on stage. It would have certainly been preferable for Maria to deal with a more intimate opera concentrated on a few characters. Perhaps conscious of her inexperience, Callas (on whose name the worldwide interest in the whole affair is concentrated, obviously) asks the Teatro Regio for permission to have Di Stefano as her co-director. In the course of the rehearsals two other "assistants" came to give a helping hand and Maria is able to concentrate her efforts primarily on the individual characters with special attention given, as would be expected, to the female lead.

Fortunately, Raina Kabaivanska, singing the part of the Duchess Elena, is a beautiful woman, an excellent actress and, above all, a Callas fan, all of which helps facilitate the progress of the rehearsals. On April 10, 1973 the première takes place after having

---

My daughter Maria was born during a great storm and today this seems symbolic to me, because from that day she never ceased to be a source of storms herself.
EVANGELIA KALOGEROPOULOS

The return. Why?

The Return

> *When she stopped singing, she thought that everything in that world had ended, that there were no more stage directors, orchestra conductors, and above all, there were no more singers. It was practically impossible to speak of music.*
> PLACIDO DOMINGO

overcome the crisis of substituting for an ill conductor, Vittorio Gui, almost ninety, who had played a large role in Callas's early career. Despite the presence of Kabaiwanska and exceptional étoiles such as Natalia Makarova and Elisabetta Terabust in the Four Seasons ballet; despite the prestige of set and costume designer Aligi Sassu, the success of the operation is not at all unanimous. The Turin experience will serve as just one more effort on Maria's part to return to that blessed stage from which she has been absent far too long. But it remained an attempt which bore no fruit.

By now it is no longer possible to postpone Maria's real appointment with the public: Di Stefano does not want it, the impresarios do not want it, the fans do not want it, and Maria does not want it. La Callas must return to singing. Well then, so be it. She and Di Stefano would perform in a program of operatic duets with piano accompaniment. If she could, if she were up to it, she would also sing solo, perhaps an encore. The announcement is made, the first dates of the tour set. London, September 22, 1973 is the fatal evening.

Nothing would come of it: eye problems crop up and the concert is postponed until November. The first notes delivered by the refurbished Callas are thus heard in Hamburg on October 25 before a hysterical audience conquered in advance just by the desire to see, hear and touch her. In the audience the most vociferous fan is Elizabeth Taylor. And Maria? What does she think, how will she overcome the agony of this test of fire awaiting her after having postponed and evaded it for eight interminable years? Where will she get the strength to walk out onto the stage?

Witnesses speak of panic in its unadulterated form, moments of blind terror. If she manages it, this is due to Di Stefano who does not leave her side for a moment, who literally leads her onto the stage by the hand. And Maria sings. How? In comparison to what she was, atrociously. Whatever the love felt for her, whatever is thought of her, her solitude, her despair, however much indulgence there is for her, what is heard is a singer beyond the limits of good and bad, a voice in shreds.

The intonation comes and goes, the breath control is often non-existent, the top notes waver perilously, the bottom notes are exaggerated chest tones. The timbre, that unmistakable Callas timbre, is unrecognizable. Is this Maria? Is this Callas, this sumptuous, beautiful woman, certainly, but obviously terrified, fragile and defenseless? For those who love her, but still do not want to renounce their lucid judgement, the Hamburg recital is a nightmare, something that one would never, ever have wanted to hear.

And under such conditions, is it absolutely certain that the delirium of the hysterical fans (yet there are some who do not applaud and the critics will be courteous, gallant and implacable) is good for her? At the moment yes, of course. But in the long run? However that may be, Maria needs that delirium like a drug, despite the fact that she is entirely lucid ("How good they are. I know perfectly well that I was rotten"). And the drug circulates, it keeps her alive. After Hamburg come Berlin and other German cities. Then Madrid. London, Paris, Amsterdam.

Milan as well, but not La Scala. Then, at the institute for cancer research where Di Stefano's daughter is hospitalized, it is performed as a private event.

With Di Stefano and Italian President Giovanni Leone after her debut as a stage director.

Evening after evening Maria gains confidence and her voice too warms up, settles down, gets started again. Now, on certain evenings, there are even beautiful moments, burning phrases, thrilling notes. Now she takes the risk of singing solo and not only the safe "O mio babbino caro" from *Gianni Schicchi*, but two, three or four arias, "Suicidio" from *La Gioconda*, Santuzza's aria, Tosca's prayer… Between February and May 1974 she gives eighteen recitals in America, at times solo, if Di Stefano should cancel. Pirate recordings immediately go circulating throughout the world.

People in cities particularly "hers" – London, Paris, Dallas, New York – go into trance on her mere appearance, shower her with torrents of love, discharge the adrenaline of pure idolatry. She is reborn, of course. But even on the best of evenings and

> *Within herself, within her voice, Callas had life itself. She had great guts as a woman and as an artist she had the fire within, but the rampant flames always alternated with moments of depression.*
> FRANCO CORELLI

in the best moments of the most successful ones, the woman who sings is not, absolutely not, Maria Callas.

Even in the most difficult moments of the early sixties, even in the half performances of

The Return

the Paris *Norma* of 1965, what was heard was the Callas voice: exhausted, lacerated, but unmistakably hers, at least in timbre, if not in substance or in its specific weight, in every accent, every inflection. Here not.

The saddest thing, what in the end will make it said that however things may have gone, however much psychological support Maria may have drawn from it, her return was a gross error, is the fact that Callas was not treated like Callas. The most important music critics in the world preferred not to write about her and whenever they may have done so they asked themselves (they asked her): Why? Her true art, her true singing, the true music was somewhere else, certainly not in these recitals. The Callas-Di Stefano recitals were an operation in nostalgia, commercial and, for Maria, an acceptance of charity. Sad when the most revolutionary singer of the century must be happy because one night she managed to sing four solo arias. Unjust when a voice that was once omnipotent must exult because for once a top note did not waver.

However, between October and November 1974 there were nine more recitals in Korea and Japan ending at Sapporo. During the course of these months, Maria has become confident enough even to consent to television filming. And so we see her, extremely tense and haughty, making the sign of the cross in her dressing room, and going on stage in a brilliant red gown, smiling, giving thanks, singing (singing?), smiling again, giving thanks again, with a sweetness and a fragility that hurt.

There is also news in her private life. An affair with Di Stefano is the obvious piece of gossip to immediately hit the press at the first announcement of their renewed partnership. The affair is immediately denied by all concerned, by their friends and collaborators, by Di Stefano's wife herself, officially on Maria's side and always with her husband in all his work engagements. In reality, the affair did take place and it was Maria's last sentimental adventure.

The motives that led her to it – she so

> *A diva among divas, empress, queen, goddess, witch, sorceress – in a word, divine. She passed through this century like a great solitary eagle whose outspread wings hid from our sight those who survived her.*
> YVES SAINT-LAURENT

intransigent, so moralistic – are easy enough to understand: loneliness, gratitude, even perhaps devotion to the man who brought her back to life, who allowed her with his mere presence to pick up the broken threads with the past, with just his energy making it possible to overcome the uncertainties, face the terrors of the challenge, the sense of inadequacy.

The fact remains that Callas-Di Stefano are a team not only on stage. She does not speak of it, and he maintains exemplary discretion. His wife too remained silent for a long time, but many years after Maria's death she published a book which, beginning from its very title names Maria as the "enemy" and smacks of an eruption too long repressed. Three months after the last date in Japan, however, Maria is a woman with projects, one of which – however senseless it may seem in retrospect – is a *Tosca* in Tokyo with Di Stefano and Gobbi. A paid visit to a cemetery of the elephants, as it were.

But in February 1975, Aristotle Onassis enters a Paris hospital and his condition soon appears to be hopeless. He dies on March 15 and for Maria it is the end of everything. Whatever may have been the state of their relationship at that moment in their respective lives, with Onassis, Maria sees the man of her life die – and not only that. With him her whole world disappears, the world in which she had a role and a function, a world that had bestowed international glory and public recognition. Maria isolates herself, her friends report that this time she really lets herself go. She seldom goes out, does not accept any social engagements, allows work proposals to drag on without being finalized, and she even neglects herself physically. She is only just fifty-two, an age at which practically all her colleagues are still at the top of their careers, yet she is a kind of relic.

On November 2, Pasolini – another father-creator figure to whom she owes one of her resurrections – is killed by a hustler on a beach at Ostia. And on March 17, 1976 just two days after the first anniversary of Onassis's death, Luchino Visconti dies in Rome, the man who more than any other allowed her to create that marvelous fusion of woman, singer, actress, legend. The old world is erased and the new one has no place for Maria.

The last part of the life of a woman who remains one of the female symbols of the twentieth century is spent in a situation of almost total solitude. Less than a month after Luchino's death, Maria interrupts the vocal training she had continued in private at the Champs-Elysées Theater. Someone photographs her clandestinely during a pause in her singing and in the newspapers appears an unflattering photo accompanied by trivial captions ("Callas cries because her voice has broken"). For Callas it is the final renunciation of any idea of future activity.

On September 16, 1977, in the late morning, Maria collapses in her bedroom. A few hours later, radio stations all over the world interrupt their broadcasts to announce the death by heart attack of "the greatest singer of the century".

THE TIME OF MEMORY

And then? And then there is an avalanche of commemorations. Front-page articles in all the dailies, page upon page of comments, photos, profiles, biographies, recollections. The passing of Maria Callas creates a great long wave. For weeks just about everyone takes up the subject, writes about her, talks about her. Inevitably there are rumors of suicide which are given credit even by some who for years have been out of touch with her, and yet who feel qualified to preside over her memory. In Italy, as in France, England, the United States, full days are dedicated to broadcasts about her. Meetings and more commemorations are organized. It will be just the beginning of a Callas avalanche that will go on for years.

Meanwhile she is cremated and buried in

I think Maria let herself die of sadness. One can really die if wants to, even without committing suicide, by abandoning life.
PLACIDO DOMINGO

Père Lachaise Cemetery. Then her ashes are stolen, rediscovered, and buried again. At last the Greek Minister of Culture, Dimitrios Nianis, disperses them over the Aegean Sea. The sarabande of memories goes on and on. Letters and notes are dug out, reports of telephone conversations (how many people claim to have received the last telephone call before her death?) confidences are invented

---

Spiritually I died with her. I want nothing else but to die physically too.
GIOVANNI BATTISTA MENEGHINI

---

and published that probably never took place. Her ex-husband enters the fray by delving into a highly personal revisiting of Maria's life ever since their separation.

False friends make their contributions (the real ones, as usual in these cases, remain silent or choose much more suitable places than the scandal pages, as it were, which is the natural destination of the former). So do colleagues, domestics, people who had never met her but who know, know everything, know something that no one else knows. The legend continues through the years. Streets and squares are named after Maria Callas the world over, as are singing competitions and musical events of all kinds. Exhibits, more or less complete, more or less honest, of her costumes, jewels, scores, stage or personal possessions, letters, notes, photos and film fragments make the rounds.

Her recordings are incessantly republished. The companies specializing in pirate editions dig up and release not only the recordings of every possible performance, but even of rehearsals. The final victory of the CD sees her discography reach ultimate completion. And that is still not enough: in order to widen the range, EMI releases some of her legendary evenings (*Anna Bolena*, of course) and goes so far as to put all previously unreleased ones on the

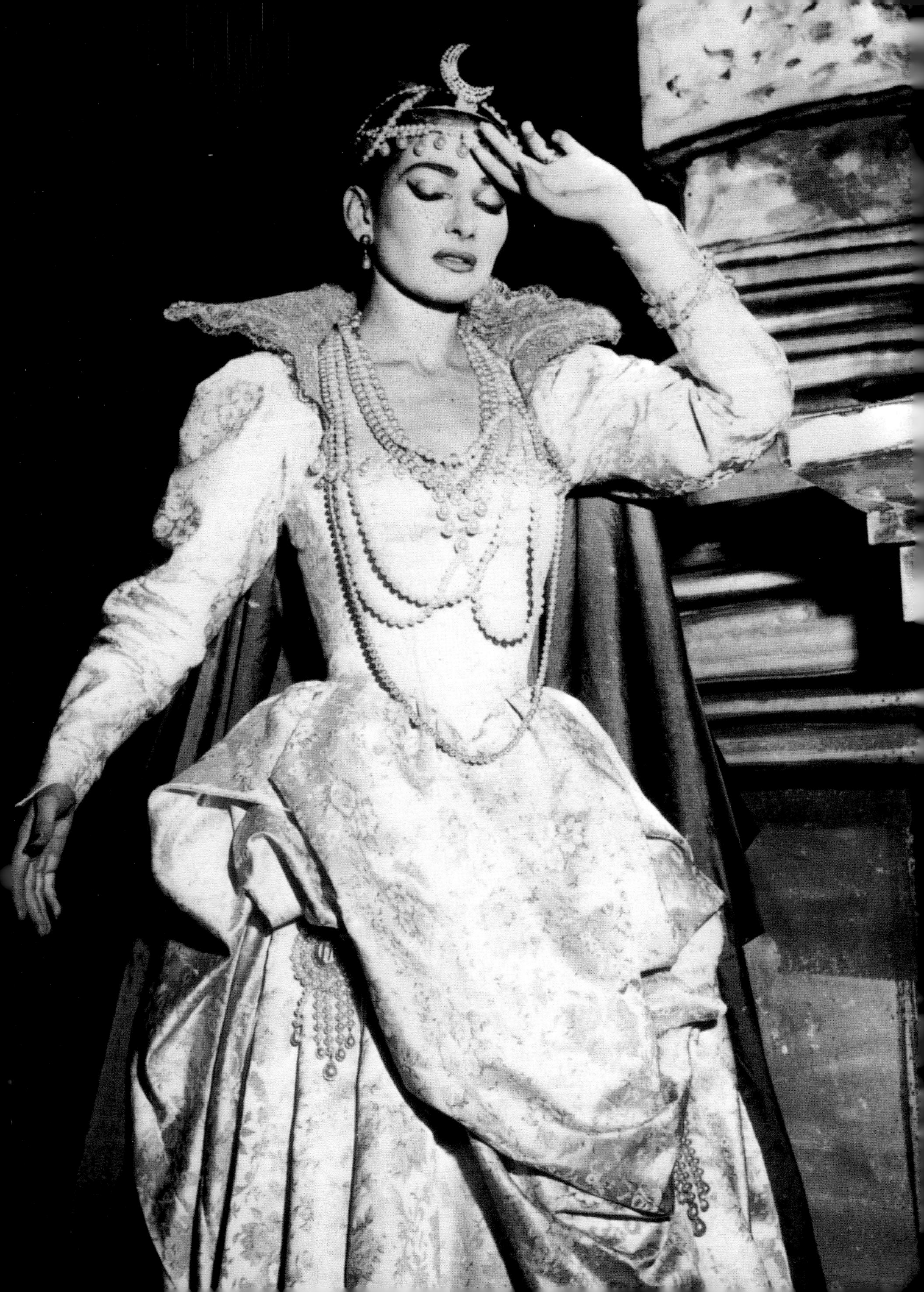

> *I feel that she killed herself,
> I feel the despair of the frustrated
> artist, the disappointed woman.*
> IRENE PAPAS

market. And which are they? Obviously all those made after 1960 which Maria herself considered unworthy – often in an excess of self-criticism, but mostly in a lucid evaluation of the results.

With the commercializing of videocassettes and CDs, more pieces go to complete the mosaic for the Callas market which unhappily and forever will be deprived of visual testimony of her great stage accomplishments. Since it is impossible to see her *Traviata*, her *Norma* or her *Bolena*, we must make do with just a few concerts, the second act of *Tosca*, performed in Paris and London; her presence at galas and some television broadcasts.

Everything is turned into a moneymaker and there are some who create film montages coming from every conceivable source: movie magazines, airport arrivals and departures, balls and charity events, whatever can help allay the hunger of the Callas fans to possess her. These are, and will continue to be, legion as we can see from the sales of everything regarding her, with ever new adepts among the younger generations.

The book market is even vaster. Year after year books of all types appear. By now there are dozens of them: critical essays of the highest level, volumes of photographs, biographies, analyses of her recordings, collections of articles. The biographical sector is doubtless the most disparate ranging from impeccable reconstructions of her life to collections of third-hand gossip: one finds literally everything. Those who collect simply everything about "la Divina", published in all languages, must by now have a special library to accomodate the material. Thus, twenty years after her death, Callas "sells" – and this, in the present market society, is perhaps the only thing that is considered.

But the truly important point is something else: it is the fact that anyone can, at any time, choose from the very many pieces she recorded, or from those recorded live by adoring fans, and hear rising from the silence of past times a voice unlike any other; that voice that shapes an accent without parallel, speaks of the pain and loneliness, passion and madness of a lacerated heart, that reverberates in empathy, annulling space and contingencies, gathering all of those who will, together in the pacification of a past regained.

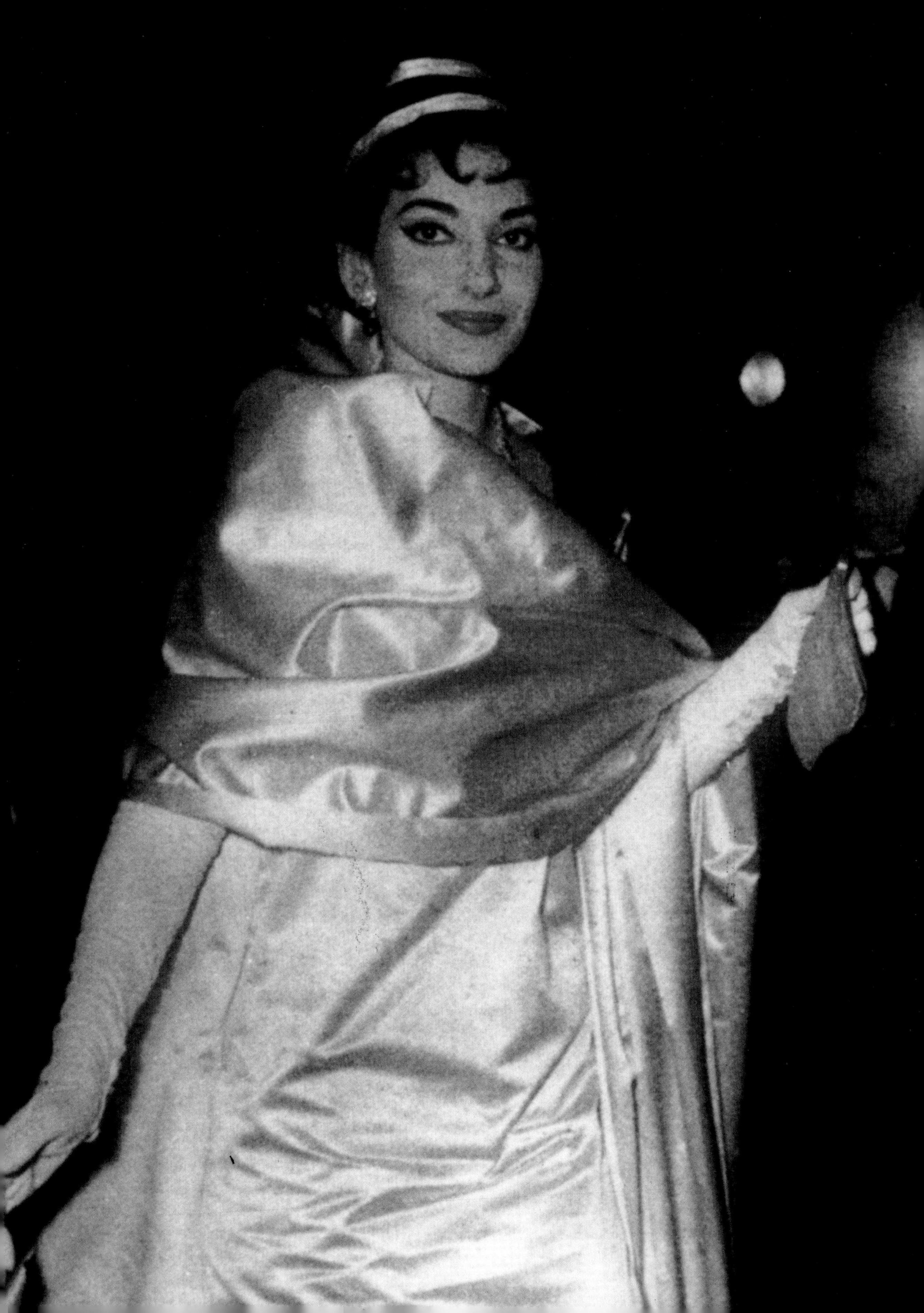

THE RECORDINGS

From September 1952 to December 1964, Maria Callas made twenty-six recordings of complete operas, twenty-two different ones (there were two versions made of *Lucia di Lammermoor, Norma, Tosca* and *La Gioconda*). Four of these operas she had never sung in the theater (*Pagliacci, Bohème, Manon Lescaut* and *Carmen*) and she would gladly have omitted recording some of them in favor of others, which were never made. Despite her prestige and repeated requests, Callas never managed to convince EMI to record operas forever linked to her name: for example *Macbeth or Il Pirata* and, above all, *Anna Bolena*.

Furthermore the recordings were not always made at the right moments (too late for*Turandot*, for instance, when she no longer sang it in the theater, whereas it would have been fine to hear her do it with the "savage" voice of her early years; and too soon for *Madam Butterfly* made before she sang it on stage) and hardly one of them was scheduled for ideal moments and working conditions.

In fact, Callas recorded mostly in Milan during the heat of August and often at the end of exhausting opera seasons. Neither did the recording schedule appear to take the needs of a human voice much into account: in 1955 the recording of *Rigoletto* followed on that of *Aida*, and two years later the recording of *Turandot* was scheduled for three days after the last performance of *Sonnambula*… True though it is that Maria made a specialty of leaping from one tessitura to another, certain follies do not leave even a "freak" voice unpunished.

The inevitable result is that not all of Callas's official recordings present her at the top of her form and that often they do not faithfully reveal the qualities of her voice at that precise moment in her artistic development.

Many witnesses, for example, agree that in 1955 or 1956, Callas in the theater had a vocal compactness, consistency and transparency that the microphone in those same years did not capture but rendered drier and more "strained". However that may be, the entire corpus of her recordings has never been out of print, and each of them has been regularly reissued, first in vinyl and later in CD.

Even more important is the fact that parallel to, and often preferable to her official recordings, pirated editions have allowed her aficionados to know and collect an impressive number of live Callas performances. Thanks to recordings made on the spot in theaters or of taped radio broadcasts, opera buffs all over the world have been able to broaden the list of the "Divina's" recordings to include *Nabucco* and *I Vespri Siciliani, Armida, Macbeth, Alceste, La Vestale, Andrea Chénier, Anna Bolena, Ifigenia, Il Pirata,* and *Poliuto*. This is without counting the other, different, often numerous editions of operas that were even recorded officially and often superior to those. The market offers five, six or seven different versions of *Norma, Lucia, Medea* or *Traviata*, real manna for the collector and precious documents for following the development through the years and according to the state of her voice of the roles to which Callas has given a special dimension.

Of course, the technical quality of these live recordings is not always good and sometimes they are not even acceptable. It matters little: their documentary value is undisputed so that in some cases where the sound is unusually good – *Traviata* in London and at La Scala, *Il Pirata* in Philadelphia, the legendary *Bolena* – EMI itself bought the pirated tapes and released those legendary performances officially, placing them in their catalog side by side with the operas Callas recorded in the studio.

In a word, the entire Callas career can be reconstructed today thanks to the live recordings transferred to CDs or the vinyl ones on the collector's market. The one unfortunate exception, her very earliest years, deprives us of the Wagnerian interpretations (only *Parsifal* exists) and some exceptional vocal exploits in the Italian repertoire. Inexplicably missing too are the tapes of some of Maria's La Scala performances from the years when every single note she uttered was already being collected by her unconditional fanatics. Thus there is nothing of her *Don Carlo*, her *Fedora*, her legendary *Pirata* with Corelli and Bastianini, unless these tapes have been put in a freezer somewhere to push up a market that is already sky-high.

With regard to excerpts, Callas recorded a little more than a hundred, including the first ones done in Turin in 1949 (Isolde's *Liebestod*, the cavatina from *Norma* and Elvira's mad scene from *I Puritani*) and the last recording of duets with Di Stefano in London in November and December of 1972. Some of these, as mentioned in preceding chapters, were released posthumously against her wishes. Collected in highly prestigious recitals (which include *Puccini Heroines*, *Callas at La Scala*, *Verdi Heroines*, *Famous Mad Scenes*, and the two-volume *Callas in Paris*) these excerpts are collected patchwork fashion on CDs that do not always respect the original compilations. Under fictitious titles these mix pieces recorded in very different periods of her career exhibit extreme variations in vocal quality according to the time in which they were made.

Nevertheless, careful checking of the dates of the recordings can certainly give an idea of the breadth of the Callas repertoire in order to hear the voice of "la divina" at various moments in her artistic development. She sings in tessituras ranging from mezzo soprano to coloratura soprano. Especially interesting in this sector too are the recitals recorded live in Europe and America, above all from the end of the fifties until 1965. Not to be missed is the recital with orchestra given in Dallas on November 21, 1957, where Callas sings arias and scenes from *The Abduction from the Seraglio*, *Puritani*, *Macbeth*, *Traviata* and *Anna Bolena*. Several labels have also released complete or partial recordings of rehearsals – documents of exceptional if rather specialized interest.

Special thanks go to the cultural organisation "Maria Callas" and to its president Bruno Tosi (P.O. Box 574, Venise, Italy, tel./fax +39/041/5237887, Website: www.callas.it) for providing many of the illustrations.

Other Gremese Titles

Enrico Stinchelli
Greatest Stars of the Opera

Stefano Masi
Roberto Benigni

Fabrizio Borin
Federico Fellini

Jen A. Gili
Italian Filmakers

Riccardo Ferrucci – Patrizia Turini
Paolo and Vittorio Taviani

Matilde Hochkofler
Marcello Mastroianni

Claudio G. Fava
Alberto Sordi

Oreste De Fornari
Sergio Leone

Stefano Masi – Enrico Lancia
Italian Movie Goddesses

Roberta Albano – Nadia Scafidi – Rita Zambon
Dance in Italy

Grazioso Cecchetti
Classical Dance (vol. I and II)